How to Cover the Catholic Church

Jerry Filteau
with Benedicta Cipolla

A resource of the
Office of Media Relations
United States Conference of Catholic Bishops

Executive Editor
Sister Mary Ann Walsh, Director
USCCB Office of Media Relations

United States Conference of Catholic Bishops
Washington, D.C.

ISBN: 978-1-60137-045-7

First Printing, April 2008

Contents

Introduction

Someone new on the religion beat.

A veteran journalist heading off to cover a story at the Vatican.

A brand new diocesan director of communications.

These and others are among the many callers who contact the Office of Media Relations of the U.S. Conference of Catholic Bishops (USCCB). Some questions are frequent:

- What's the Vatican phone number? (It's 011-39-06-6982.)
- How does a coadjutor bishop differ from an auxiliary bishop? (The former has the right of succession, for one thing.)
- Do you need to be divorced to get an annulment? (Yes.)

These people and such questions led us to commission this resource, *How to Cover the Catholic Church*. It's for journalists—to make their work easier; it's for the church—to facilitate better coverage; it's for anyone who wants to know a little more of the inner workings of the Catholic Church.

The principal writer was Jerry Filteau, a veteran journalist who spent 35 years covering the church for Catholic News Service. With experience in Rome and in Washington, Jerry has covered papal travels to five continents, more than 40 national meetings of the U.S. bishops, the deaths and elections of popes from Pope Paul VI onwards, and everything in between. He knows the complicated and makes the complicated known to whoever can read a newspaper. With Jerry on this project, we knew we were in good hands.

Assisting him was Benedicta Cipolla, a young writer and quick study who worked in Rome from 1995 to 2001. She spent more than two years at the Catholic News Service Rome Bureau and Vatican Radio, the incredible station which reaches around the world. A little bit of Rome experience goes a long way, for, indeed, all roads do lead to Rome and anyone who ever has worked there comes away a different, and often deeper, person.

Many people assisted in this work. The CNS Rome Bureau proofed the Vatican section; Jerry regularly called on staff at the USCCB to verify information on the bishops' conference and spoke with canon lawyers about some of the entries involving issues of church law. Meanwhile, USCCB Publishing gave a yeoman's effort in designing and editing, even as they prepared for the first visit of Pope Benedict XVI to the United States, slated for April 15-20, 2008.

The USCCB's Secretary for Communications, Helen Osman, was a strong leader and enthusiastic backer of the project, and the Catholic Communication Campaign agreed to fund it as a way of improving media coverage of the church—a key goal.

We in Media Relations hope this work helps you. We offer a special prayer that it does, for your work as a journalist is noble, a service to all who search for truth in their newspapers, on the Web and in their souls.

Sister Mary Ann Walsh, RSM
Director of Media Relations
USCCB

Covering the Vatican

If you're reading this, your editor probably just (a) assigned you to cover a papal trip or an event at the Vatican, or (b) asked you to get comments from Rome regarding a local issue in which Holy See policy might come into play. Headed by the pope, the Holy See is the central authority of the Catholic Church. Technically it differs from the Vatican, which refers to the independent state established by the Lateran Pact with Italy in 1929 as Vatican City State, the smallest sovereign nation in the world. As noted, Vatican City State is distinct from the Holy See, which refers to the pope and his Curia.

Just as the U.S. president has a cabinet of officials overseeing various areas of national government, the pope has the Roman Curia, which oversees the various facets of church life around the world. Familiarity with the Curia and knowing which departments focus on which facets are extremely helpful in tackling any story concerning the Vatican, since knowing whom to contact can be half the battle. If you're about to book a plane ticket for Rome, there are several types of events you might be covering; and before you go it's wise to get a handle on what to expect, be it a canonization ceremony, your local archbishop receiving his pallium, or the election of a new pope (not to mention the process of actually getting accredited to cover the event). Outside the Curia itself, there are many resources to help you get acquainted—from the official Vatican newspaper and other publications to the American seminary in Rome. Whatever your assignment, the following information should help get you started.

PRESS CREDENTIALS

If you're traveling to Rome, apply ahead of time for temporary accreditation to the Press Office of the Holy See (*Sala Stampa della Santa Sede*). You can survive without it, but it makes covering events easier, and the press office itself can be a useful resource.

Print journalists will need the following:

1. An accreditation form. This can be filled out online. Go to *www.vatican.va/news_services/index.htm* and click on Accreditation.
2. A formal written request for accreditation from an editor or someone in a managerial position at your news organization, on company letterhead. The request should state
   - The time period and event or story for which accreditation is being requested.
   - That you're a professional journalist assigned to cover said event or story.
   - That you will respect ethical norms such as embargoes.
3. A photocopy of your press identification card, if you have one.
4. A photocopy of your passport.
5. One passport-sized color photograph.

After you have submitted the online form, e-mail documents 2-5 to *accreditamenti@pressva.va*. This address is only used for accreditation.

You can also fax them (except for the photograph) to 39-06-686-8810. (Note: 39 is the country code for Italy; 06 is the area code for Rome and Vatican City and is required even for local calls. Most local numbers in Rome or the Vatican are 10 digits now, but some older ones are still nine digits or fewer. Phone or fax numbers given here do not include initial international access; it's 011 from the United States.)

Or mail them to:

Holy See Press Office
Accreditation Office
Via della Conciliazione 54
SCV-00120 CITTÀ DEL VATICANO

The main press office telephone number is 39-06-698-921, and the accreditation office hours are from 11 a.m. to 1 p.m., Monday through Friday. Rome is six hours ahead of the East Coast most of the year. (It is only five hours ahead for a brief period each spring and fall because the United States begins daylight saving time before Europe does and ends it after Europe does.)

Once in Rome, proceed to the press office between 11 a.m. and 1 p.m. with copies of all the documents already submitted (print a copy of the accreditation form, too), plus an extra passport-sized photograph, just in case something's missing. Do not be surprised or alarmed if your pass isn't ready on your first trip to the press office. Patience will be rewarded.

TV crews and still photographers go through a similar process via the Pontifical Council for Social Communications rather than the Vatican press office.

In the press accreditation section of the Vatican's Web site (*www.vatican. va/news_services/press/accred/index_en.htm*), click on Audiovisual Permits and fill out the online form. Note that each person requesting accreditation must complete the form.

Then fax (39-06-6988-5373) or e-mail a formal written request from the TV organization or photo agency along with the name(s) and title(s) of the people requiring accreditation, and a photocopy of each person's passport.

Once in Rome, go to the main office of the council at Via della Conciliazione n. 5, a few blocks down from St. Peter's Square. Bring photocopies of all the documents requested, and be sure to have your passport on hand for identification.

The council's office publishes regulations for audiovisual coverage at the Vatican and rules of conduct at papal ceremonies. Links can be found at *www. vatican.va/roman_curia/pontifical_councils/pccs/av-pccs/Accreditamento_ AV_en.htm*. Read these before applying for accreditation to make sure you can comply, and take them with you as a reference.

Keep your press pass visible at all times when covering events. The press office will provide a clear plastic sleeve to wear on a lanyard around your neck. Note that the pass will get you into events, but it won't get you past the gates behind St. Peter's unless you have an appointment.

The Press Office (*Sala Stampa*)

Conveniently located on Via della Conciliazione, the street leading to St. Peter's, and just outside the square itself, the office provides wi-fi, electrical outlets, phones, copies of daily press releases and other documents, and a (not always very quiet) place to work. If your laptop somehow didn't survive the trip, there are five first-come, first-served computers, all with Internet access and connection to a printer. The press office is also where most of the major press conferences are held. TV crews and still photographers should check in with the Pontifical Council for Social Communications ahead of any press conference to determine who gets a spot, since audiovisual hookups are at a premium. Official Vatican photos and television footage will be made available in any event. For those filing radio reports, the press office has fairly sound-proof phone booths.

To obtain television footage, contact the Vatican Television Center, known by its Italian acronym as CTV. The director general is Jesuit Father Federico Lombardi, who also heads the press office. Phone 06-6988-5467 or 5233. E-mail *ctv@ctv.va* (main office) or *ctvteca@ctv.va* (archive). For photographs of the pope and Vatican events, go to *www.photo.va*, the Web site of Vatican newspaper's photo service. Phone 06-6988-4797. E-mail *photo@ossrom.va*.

Every day around noon, the press office releases the *Bollettino*, or daily bulletin (plural: *Bollettini*). If you're in the building, you'll hear an announcement of its arrival over the loudspeaker, at which point all the reporters form a scrum near the entrance to grab a copy. Depending on the day and the expected content, the scrum may be calm or frenzied, but there are always plenty of bulletins to go around. More than one *Bollettino* is usually released per day. If you miss a day, there are back copies from the previous week or so on display.

The *Bollettino* is where you'll find out whom the pope might have met that day (*Le Udienze*) and which bishops resigned or were appointed or transferred (*Rinunce e Nomine*). On Wednesdays you'll get the text of the pope's general audience (*Udienza Generale*), and on Sundays the text of the prayer after the *Angelus* (*Preghiera dopo l'Angelus*). Papal speeches to visiting dignitaries, clergy and various groups; official messages to the United Nations and other entities; and statements from the chief Vatican spokesperson, Jesuit Father Federico Lombardi, can also be found here. The *Bollettino* is nearly always in Italian but sometimes includes other languages. If you're covering an event at the Vatican for a short period of time, such as the elevation of your city's bishop to cardinal, the *Bollettino* may be provided in or translated into English.

Bollettini are also available online, under the press office section of the Vatican's Web site. You'll note the Web site offers an archive of *Bollettini*, going back to 1997. You can search by date or by category: episcopal nominations, audiences, press releases, messages, and travels. With a press pass you can get access to the *Bollettini* under embargo on the site as well; ask at the press office about getting a password.

Be advised of the hours of operation: 9 a.m. to 3 p.m. Monday through Friday, 9 a.m. to 2 p.m. Saturday, and 11 a.m. to 1 p.m. Sundays and holidays. Holidays include obvious ones like January 1, and others you may not think of, like November 1 (Solemnity of All Saints), December 8 (Solemnity of the Immaculate Conception), and August 15 (Solemnity of the Assumption). For some special events and under extraordinary circumstances (a papal transition, for example), the press office will keep longer hours. Open hours of the press office are usually reduced during summer months and around Christmas and Easter.

THE HOLY SEE VS. VATICAN CITY STATE

The official name of the independent state established by the Lateran Pact with Italy in 1929 is Vatican City State. The name should be used only when referring to the local civil administration or its agencies—a fairly rare occurrence. At 108.7 acres, it is the smallest sovereign nation in the world and is distinct from the Holy See, which refers to the pope and his Curia.

The Holy See exercises sovereignty over Vatican City State, however. The pope, as head of the Holy See, has full legislative, judicial and executive powers, but the secretary of state acts as the pope's representative in all matters relating to the civil state. A governor, under the supervision of the Pontifical Commission for Vatican City State, administers Vatican City State. The agencies that handle Vatican stamps and coins, the post office, and the Vatican monuments and museums are all part of the civil government offices. You can find more information at *www.vaticanstate.va*.

In discussion of the central offices of the Catholic Church in their global role of authority and service, *the Vatican* has come to be interchangeable with *the Holy See* in popular speech and in news reporting. In most news contexts *Vatican* has become the term of choice. Be careful, however, about using *the Vatican* as a blanket term when instead an individual should be cited. For example, if the head of the Congregation for the Clergy speaks at a news conference, attribute the comments to him in his role as a Vatican official, not to the Vatican in general.

THE ROMAN CURIA

A *dicastery* is a major Vatican department or administrative office. The dicasteries as a whole are called the *Roman Curia*. The most common dicasteries you may encounter as a reporter are listed below, along with the leaders of each dicastery as of spring 2008. The Secretariat of State and Vatican congregations are usually headed by a cardinal, with bishops, priests, religious, and laypeople working below him; pontifical councils may be headed by a cardinal or an archbishop. The head of a congregation is called the *prefect*; the head of a pontifical council is called the *president*.

The Vatican maintains sections on its Web site for each dicastery. They contain general information and certain documents, but not everything has been translated into English, and contact information is in most cases conspicuously absent. The home page of the Vatican Web site is *www.vatican.va*. After choosing your language, you'll find links to information on popes, curial departments and other offices, liturgical celebrations, news services and more.

Most curial offices generally are open from 9 a.m. to 1:30 p.m., Monday through Saturday. On Tuesdays and Fridays they reopen from about 5 to 7 p.m. If you can't locate a direct telephone number, dial 06-6982—yes, a six-digit number—for the main Vatican switchboard, which will direct your call.

Note: For simplicity, this phone number and others given in the rest of this chapter are just the local numbers, without the country prefix, 39, required for calling from outside Italy. From the United States, the full prefix for direct-dial long-distance access to the Vatican is 011-39.

More details about every Curia department can be found in the *Annuario Pontificio*, or Vatican yearbook, published annually and available at the Vatican bookstore and other shops around St. Peter's. This little red book—it's almost 2,500 pages, but only seven inches tall and five inches wide—includes demographic and contact information on church jurisdictions worldwide, short biographical information on every bishop, a list of past popes, and information on the current pope, the College of Cardinals, religious orders, Catholic schools and cultural institutions, papal diplomats, and the diplomatic corps to the Holy See. It's an invaluable resource for someone who regularly needs this type of information and must contact a wide variety of church officials, but probably unnecessary for someone who covers the Vatican only occasionally. For anyone first learning to use the *Annuario*, Catholic News Service's *CNS Stylebook on Religion* has a helpful appendix on how to use it, including English meanings of the Italian abbreviations and English translations of departmental names, religious titles and job descriptions.

Secretariat of State

This is the most important curial department, and the secretary of state is considered the most important position at the Vatican after the pope. The secretariat is responsible for dealing with the Roman Curia as well as overseeing the Vatican's diplomatic and political activity. Its Section for General Affairs oversees internal church matters, including curial appointments; administers Vatican communication agencies; handles all Vatican documents; and acts as a liaison to embassies accredited to the Holy See. The Section for Relations with States is responsible for the Holy See's diplomatic relations with other countries.

The secretary of state is Cardinal Tarcisio Bertone. The secretary for relations with states (foreign minister) is Archbishop Dominique Mamberti. The undersecretary for relations with states is Msgr. Pietro Parolin. For the secre-

tary of state's office: phone 06-6988-3913; e-mail *vatio26@relstat-segstat.va*.
For general affairs: phone 06-6988-3438; e-mail *vatio23@genaff-segstat.va*.
For foreign affairs: phone 06-6988-3014; e-mail *vatio32@relstat-segstat.va.*

Congregation for the Doctrine of the Faith

The oldest of the Curia's congregations, the doctrinal office was founded
in 1542 as the Holy Roman and Universal Inquisition. The Inquisition got
dropped from the name in 1908, and Pope Paul VI bestowed the current
name in 1965. According to a document from Pope John Paul II, its duty
is "to promote and safeguard the doctrine on faith and morals in the whole
Catholic world" (*Pastor Bonus*, no. 48). It is divided into three sections: the
doctrinal office, the disciplinary office and the matrimonial office. The congregation is responsible for publishing doctrinal material (the 2000 document
Dominus Iesus or the 2007 position on artificial nutrition and hydration, for
example), investigating the writings of others for possible errors, taking disciplinary action (including cases of clerical sexual abuse), and making some
marriage decisions.

The prefect of the Congregation for the Doctrine of the Faith also presides
over the **Pontifical Biblical Commission** and the **International Theological
Commission**. They are groups of biblical and theological experts, respectively, from around the world who are called on by the congregation or the
pope as consultants on biblical or theological issues. Each commission has a
yearly plenary meeting in Rome. The theological commission is a bit more
prolific than the biblical commission in issuing documents on various themes.
In 2007 it released a noteworthy commentary critiquing the traditional con-
cept of limbo, saying there was good reason to hope that babies who die without being baptized go to heaven.

The congregation's prefect is an American, Cardinal William J. Levada. Its
secretary is Archbishop Angelo Amato. The undersecretary, also an American,
is Dominican Father J. Augustine Di Noia. The promoter of justice is Msgr.
Charles Scicluna. E-mail *cdf@cfaith.va*. Phone 06-6988-3357 or 3413.

The biblical commission's secretary is Jesuit Father Klemens Stock. E-mail
pcombiblica@cfaith.va. Phone 06-6988-4682. The theological commission's
secretary general is Jesuit Father Luis F. Ladaria. Phone 06-6988-4727.

Congregation for Eastern Churches

This is a kind of super-congregation for all matters pertaining to the Eastern
Catholic churches, in their original homelands and wherever they have

spread around the world, including the United States, Canada, Latin America, Western Europe and Australia. It covers the same terrain for those churches that the congregations for bishops, clergy, Catholic education and religious cover for the Catholic Church's Latin rite majority. The agency also deals with jurisdictional questions and administrative issues in those churches.

While in full communion with Rome, meaning they accept the primacy of the pope, the 22 Eastern Catholic churches retain their own liturgical traditions and legal systems. In most Eastern churches married men may be ordained priests but often only in the original homeland of their church—Asia, Eastern Europe or North Africa—not in the West. Bishops must be celibate. Synods have authority to make decisions, such as electing bishops and patriarchs and erecting dioceses.

The congregation oversees the Vatican's coordinating body of aid agencies for Eastern churches, known by its Italian acronym, ROACO. In addition it supervises the Catholic Near East Welfare Association, which provides humanitarian and pastoral support for churches of the Middle East, North Africa, India and Eastern Europe; and also the Pontifical Mission for Palestine, a relief and development agency for the Middle East. Headquarters for both are in New York. For more information on both entities, see the next chapter, under "Vatican or Vatican-Related Organizations and Agencies."

The prefect is Cardinal Leonardo Sandri. The secretary is Archbishop Antonio Maria Vegliò. The undersecretary is Msgr. Krzysztof Nitkiewicz. Phone 06-6988-4293. E-mail *cco@orientchurch.va.*

The president of the Catholic Near East Welfare Association is Cardinal Edward M. Egan of New York. Its secretary general is Msgr. Robert L. Stern, who is also president of the Pontifical Mission for Palestine. E-mail *cnewa@ cnewa.org* or *pmp@cnewa.org.* Phone (in New York) 212-826-1480.

Congregation for Divine Worship and the Discipline of the Sacraments

This congregation oversees liturgical issues like the compilation, translation and adaptation of liturgical books and rites, as well as norms for the celebration of the liturgy around the world. It's also responsible for determining the validity of ordinations in certain cases and deals with some matters concerning marriage, though not annulments.

The prefect is Cardinal Francis Arinze. The secretary is Archbishop Albert Malcolm Ranjith Patabendige Don (*Archbishop Ranjith* on second reference).

The undersecretary is Marist Father Anthony Ward. E-mail *cultdiv@ccdds.va*. Phone 06-6988-4316, 4318 or 4326.

In 2001 the congregation formed a *Vox Clara* Committee, composed of English-speaking bishops, as consultants on the English translation of the Mass. The Latin phrase in the name means "clear voice." U.S. members are Cardinals Francis E. George of Chicago and Justin Rigali of Philadelphia and Archbishops Alfred C. Hughes of New Orleans and Oscar H. Lipscomb of Mobile, Ala.

Congregation for the Causes of Saints

This congregation investigates all those being considered for official church recognition as saints. It makes recommendations to the pope on beatifications and canonizations and oversees the authentication and preservation of sacred relics.

The prefect is Cardinal José Saraiva Martins. The secretary is Archbishop Michele Di Ruberto. The undersecretary is Msgr. Marcello Bartolucci. The promoter of the faith is Msgr. Sandro Corradini. Phone 06-6988-4247.

Congregation for Bishops

This congregation oversees bishops' appointments, bishops' conferences, and *ad limina* visits (official visits to Rome by bishops every five years). Personal prelatures like Opus Dei, which do not report to a diocesan bishop, and military ordinaries (bishops responsible for the pastoral care of Catholics in the armed forces) also fall under its authority.

The prefect is Cardinal Giovanni Battista Re. The secretary is Archbishop Francesco Monterisi. The undersecretary is Msgr. Giovanni Maria Rossi. Phone 06-6988-4217.

Congregation for the Evangelization of Peoples

Once called *Propaganda Fide*, or propagation of the faith, the evangelization congregation coordinates the missionary work of Catholic Church. The office manages pastoral outreach, charitable activity, fund raising and ministry in mission territories, which include Africa, most of Asia and Oceania, and dioceses in Latin America, Canada, Alaska, the Balkans and the Caucasus. It also fulfills in mission territories the functions handled by the congregations for bishops and clergy in the rest of the Latin Church.

Four pontifical missionary societies operate under the direction of the evangelization congregation: the Societies of St. Peter Apostle and the

Propagation of the Faith, the Holy Childhood Association, and the Missionary Union of Priests and Religious. The agencies promote missionary awareness and support fund raising for the church's activity in mission lands.

A useful news service, Fides, also operates under the congregation. See the "Resources" section in this chapter for more information.

The prefect of the evangelization congregation is Cardinal Ivan Dias. Its secretary is Archbishop Robert Sarah. Its undersecretary is Father Massimo Cenci. Phone 06-6987-1523. E-mail *segreteria@propagandafide.va*.

Congregation for Clergy

This congregation oversees the ongoing spiritual, intellectual and pastoral formation of diocesan priests and deacons and most matters affecting their pastoral ministry, including issues of compensation, medical care, disability and pensions. It also oversees the religious education of the faithful of all ages and the administration of church property.

The prefect is Cardinal Claudio Hummes. The secretary is Archbishop Mauro Piacenza. The undersecretary is Msgr. Giovanni Carrù. Phone 06-6988-4151. E-mail *clero@cclergy.va*.

Congregation for Institutes of Consecrated Life and Societies of Apostolic Life

This congregation oversees all church-recognized institutes of consecrated life— the term used for religious orders and congregations of men or women and for secular institutes of men or women—and societies of men or women who devote their lives to some particular apostolate or aspect of the church's mission.

The prefect is Cardinal Franc Rodé. The secretary is Archbishop Gianfranco Gardin. There are two undersecretaries: Salesian Sister Enrica Rosanna, the highest-ranking woman at the Vatican; and Cistercian Father Sebastiano Paciolla, a priest of the Missionary Servants of the Poor. Phone 06-6988-4128. E-mail *civcsva.pref@ccscrlife.va* (prefect), *civcsva.segr@ccscrlife.va* (secretary), or *vati059@ccscrlife.va* (general e-mail).

Congregation for Catholic Education

This dicastery has authority over Catholic seminaries, colleges and universities, elementary and secondary schools and other educational institutes around the world, except for those under the authority of the Congregation for Eastern Churches. It has special authority over ecclesiastical schools or faculties around the world—those specifically licensed by the Holy See to grant ecclesiastical (as distinct from civil) degrees. Those schools cannot appoint a rector or dean or full professor without confirmation by the congregation, and it must approve anyone nominated by those schools for an honorary degree.

The prefect is Cardinal Zenon Grocholewski. The secretary is Bishop Jean-Louis Brugues. The undersecretary is Msgr. Angelo Zani. Phone 06-6988-4167.

Vatican Court System

As part of the Catholic Church's court, or tribunal, system, the Vatican has three central tribunals.

Apostolic Penitentiary

This is a Vatican court dealing with indulgences and the sacrament of penance and reconciliation. For example, in 2007, the court announced a special indulgence for Catholics who took part in certain devotions to Our Lady of Lourdes, to mark the 150th anniversary of Mary's appearance to Bernadette Soubirous, a girl who lived in southern France. The *major penitentiary*, or head of the court, is the pope's delegate in hearing petitions for forgiveness from people guilty of sins reserved to the Holy See. The office also sponsors seminars on the sacrament of penance, of which confession is a part, and commissions priests to serve as confessors in Rome's four patriarchal basilicas.

The major penitentiary is an American, Cardinal James Francis Stafford. The regent is Father Gianfranco Girotti. Phone 06-6988-7526. E-mail *reggente@ apostpnt.va*.

Supreme Tribunal of the Apostolic Signature

Also simply called the *Apostolic Signature* (or, on second reference, *the Signature*), this is the church's supreme court. You may also hear canon lawyers or others refer to it by its name in Italian, *Segnatura*, or in Latin, *Signatura*. It is an appeals court, hearing challenges to lower court judgments or to decisions by Vatican offices and local bishops—especially appeals based on claims that the lower court or official failed to follow proper canonical procedures in reaching the decision. The court's prefect is the Vatican's second-highest legal authority, after the pope. According to norms revised by Pope John Paul II, particularly serious crimes against morals and the sacraments, such as sexual abuse of a minor by a cleric, are reserved to the Congregation for the Doctrine of the Faith, whose decisions in those cases may not be appealed to the Signature.

The prefect is Cardinal Agostino Vallini. The secretary is Bishop Velasio De Paolis. Phone 06-6988-7520.

Roman Rota

The Roman Rota is the main central appeals court of the church. Most of its docket is made up of marriage annulment cases that have first gone through diocesan tribunals. Twenty judges, called *auditors*, sit on the court. They usually hear cases in a three-person panel. Only the Apostolic Signature can vacate a Rota decision. Typically a marriage case is first decided in a diocesan tribunal. If it finds a marriage null, its decision is then reviewed by the metropolitan or regional tribunal that has appellate jurisdiction over that diocese, because the church requires two concordant decisions for a declaration of nullity. If the second court reverses the first court's verdict, the case goes to the Rota for a final decision. Sometimes, however, a party in the case may appeal the diocesan verdict directly to the Rota. Certain cases, such as those involving a governor or head of state, are automatically reserved to the Rota's jurisdiction as the court of first trial; in those cases, a second panel of judges on the Rota reviews the decision of the first panel.

The dean of the Rota is Bishop Antoni Stankiewicz. Phone 06-6988-7502.

Pontifical Council for the Laity

This council was formed after Vatican II to promote the participation of laypeople in the life and mission of the church. It oversees preparations for World Youth Day, an annual event that typically draws hundreds of thousands of Catholic young people from many nations, and a wide range of lay Catholic movements devoted to spiritual renewal or various apostolic works. A layperson is a Catholic who is not ordained.

The council's president is Cardinal Stanislaw Rylko. Its secretary is Bishop Josef Clemens. The undersecretary is Guzmán Carriquiry Lecour (*Carriquiry* on 2nd reference.) Phone 06-6988-7322, 7141, 7396, 7333 or 7296. E-mail *pcpl@laity.va*.

Pontifical Council for Promoting Christian Unity

The Christian unity council was created as a Vatican secretariat by Pope John XXIII in 1960 in preparation for the Second Vatican Council, and it played a central role in formulating the council's *Decree on Christian Unity* and its *Declaration on the Relationship of the Church to Non-Christian Religions*. The council—its name was changed from *Secretariat* to *Pontifical Council* in 1988—is the Vatican agency directly responsible for Catholic representation in numerous international bilateral theological dialogues with other Christian churches or ecclesial communities, and for multilateral Catholic relations with the World Council of Churches and other multi-denominational groups such as the Lutheran World Federation and the World Alliance of Reformed Churches. It also monitors and collaborates in the work of many national or regional ecumenical dialogues and fosters a variety of other forms of communication and collaboration with other Christian churches and ecclesial communions. The council is engaged in international theological dialogue with the following:

- The Orthodox Churches
- The Oriental Orthodox Churches
- The Malankara Churches
- The Anglican Communion
- The Lutheran World Federation
- The World Alliance of Reformed Churches
- The World Methodist Council
- The Baptist World Alliance
- The Christian Church (Disciples of Christ)
- Some Pentecostal groups

The council's section on the Vatican's Web site includes extensive documentation of those dialogues and other developments in Catholic ecumenical relations. In 1974 Pope Paul VI established the **Commission for Religious Relations with the Jews**, distinct from the council but under its aegis.

Cardinal Walter Kasper is president of both the council and the commission. Bishop Brian Farrell is secretary of the council and vice president of the commission. The council's undersecretary is Msgr. Eleuterio Francesco Fortino. The commission's secretary is Salesian Father Norbert Hofmann. Phone 06-6988-3072 or 4083. E-mail *office1@chrstuni.va*.

Pontifical Council for the Family

Responsible for pastoral ministry to families, this council promotes strong Christian marriage, family life, and responsible procreation and coordinates initiatives in defense of human life from conception to natural death. Among issues it addresses—often in conjunction with other dicasteries such as the Congregation for the Doctrine of the Faith—are natural family planning, marriage preparation, sex education, demographics, contraception, abortion, sterilization, bioethics issues and legislation regarding marriage, family, and the protection of human life. Council members include 29 married couples.

The president is Cardinal Alfonso López Trujillo. The secretary is Msgr. Grzegorz Kaszak. There is no current undersecretary. Phone 06-6988-7243. E-mail *pcf@family.va*.

Pontifical Council for Justice and Peace

This council promotes peace, justice and human rights around the world in the light of the Gospel and of the social teaching of the Church. It participates in many international meetings where such issues are discussed and analyzed and sponsors many such meetings itself. It issues documents on the moral and ethical dimensions of current issues such as international debt, racism, the arms trade and land distribution.

The council's president is Cardinal Renato Martino. Bishop Giampaolo Crepaldi is secretary. There is no current undersecretary. Phone 06-6987-9911. E-mail *pcjustpax@justpeace.va*.

Pontifical Council *Cor Unum*

Cor Unum—Latin for "one heart"—is the Vatican's charity arm, assisting the pope with disaster relief and other humanitarian aid. It is also responsible for promoting and coordinating Catholic charitable activity. The council disburses donations from the faithful, which in 2006 totaled about $8 million.

Operating under the auspices of *Cor Unum* is *Caritas Internationalis*, an international confederation of Catholic Charities agencies and international relief organizations, such as Catholic Relief Services. *Cor Unum* also oversees two foundations begun by Pope John Paul II: the Foundation for the Sahel, which funds projects to combat drought and desertification in Africa; and the *Populorum Progressio* Foundation, for farmworkers and the indigenous peoples of Latin America and the Caribbean. The latter gets its name from the Latin title of Pope Paul VI's 1967 social encyclical, *The Progress of Peoples*.

The president is Cardinal Paul Josef Cordes. The secretary is Msgr. Karel Kasteel. The undersecretary is Msgr. Giovanni Pietro Dal Toso. Phone 06-6988-9411. E-mail *corunum@corunum.va*.

Pontifical Council for Migrants and Travelers

This council primarily occupies itself with migrants and refugees, but circus and carnival workers, tourists, pilgrims, and nomadic people like the Rom (Gypsies) are also part of its mission. In 2007 the council hosted the Vatican's first international conference addressing the pastoral needs of the homeless.

The president is Cardinal Renato Martino. The secretary is Archbishop Agostino Marchetto and the undersecretary is Msgr. Novatus Rugambwa. Phone 06-6988-7193 or 7242. E-mail *office@migrants.va*.

Pontifical Council for Health Care Ministry

The health care council is entrusted with a range of functions. It not only encourages the work of hospital chaplains and Catholics working in the health care industry, but also provides guidance on technological advances and policy positions, defends the right of Catholic medical personnel to object to participation in procedures they find immoral, and lobbies pharmaceutical companies to lower prices of medications. In its work with religious and secular health care associations and with global initiatives like the United Nations' World Health Organization, the council emphasizes both physical and spiritual well-being and the inviolable dignity of the human person from conception to natural death.

Pope John Paul II, who founded the health care agency first as a pontifical commission, also instituted a World Day for the Sick, which is celebrated every year on February 11, the feast of Our Lady of Lourdes.

Cardinal Javier Lorenzo Barragan is council president. The secretary is Bishop José Redrado Marchite. The undersecretary is Missionaries of St. Joseph Father Felice Ruffini. Phone 06-6988-3138 or 4720. E-mail *opersanit@hlthwork.va*.

Pontifical Council for Legislative Texts

This council interprets canon law and ensures that documents and decrees from other Vatican offices and bishops' conferences conform to the legal norms of the church. While much of its work may lie beyond the purview of most reporters, in 2005 the council released *Dignitas Connubii*, a handbook of procedures for accepting, investigating, judging and appealing marriage cases.

The president is Archbishop Francesco Coccopalmerio. The vice president is Archbishop Bruno Bertagna. The secretary is Msgr. Juan Arrieta Ochoa. The undersecretary is an American, Msgr. Bernard A. Hebda. Phone 06-6988-4008.

Pontifical Council for Interreligious Dialogue

Another post-Vatican II council, this agency promotes dialogue between the Catholic Church and other religions. Religious leaders visiting the Vatican often make a stop here. As part of Pope Benedict XVI's response to an open letter from Muslim scholars in 2007, he invited them to meet with him and the council. Issues on the church's radar include religious freedom and reciprocity in recognizing the rights of Christians and Muslims in countries where either group is a minority.

Under its aegis is the **Commission for Religious Relations with Muslims**, which works specifically to promote greater understanding and cooperation between Catholics and Muslims.

Cardinal Jean-Louis Tauran is president of the council and the commission. Archbishop Pier Luigi Celata is council secretary and commission vice president. There is no council undersecretary currently. Msgr. Khaled Akasheh is commission secretary. Phone 06-6988-4321. E-mail *dialogo@interrel.va*.

Pontifical Council for Culture

Pope John Paul II founded the culture council in 1982, but its roots go back to the Second Vatican Council's *Pastoral Constitution on the Church in the Modern World, Gaudium et Spes*. The council promotes the Gospel's engagement with contemporary cultures, examines the rift between the Gospel and various cultural milieus, encourages the study of unbelief and religious indifference and engages in dialogue with non-believers. Pope Benedict XVI has made the challenge of secularism a hallmark of his papacy and has cast dialogue with Islam and other religions as a dialogue of cultures and civilizations in cooperation against secular society. The council has long worked closely with the interreligious dialogue office, at times overseeing it. Recent conferences sponsored by the council in Rome and around the world have included "The Presence and Absence of Christians in Art" and "20th Century Literature and Catholicism." In addition the council manages the pontifical academies.

The pontifical academies you'll most likely need to keep in mind are the **Academy of Sciences**, the **Academy of Social Sciences**, and the **Academy**

for Life. Each is nonsectarian and, although associated with the Vatican, operates autonomously. Each academy is made up of a small central office and dozens of members, all named to their positions by the pope. Most are university professors, of whom several are American. You can find a list of members in the *Annuario*.

The council president is Archbishop Gianfranco Ravasi. The secretary is Norbertine Father Bernard Ardura. The undersecretary is Msgr. Melchor Sánchez de Toca y Alameda. 06-6989-3811. E-mail *cultura@cultura.va*.

The president of the Academy of Sciences is Nicola Cabibbo. Phone 06-6988-3195. E-mail *academy.sciences@acdscience.va*.

The presidency of the Academy of Social Sciences is currently vacant. Phone 06-6988-1441. E-mail *social.sciences@acdscience.va*.

The president of the Academy for Life is Bishop Elio Sgreccia. Phone 06-6988-1693. E-mail *pav@acdlife.va*. The Web address is *www.academiavita.org*.

Pontifical Council for Social Communications

This council does more than just grant accreditation to broadcast journalists as described earlier. It also organizes World Communications Day, supports media with a distinct Catholic identity and presents an annual film prize at the Venice Film Festival. It has issued documents promoting ethical standards in advertising, in communications and on the Internet. Another council document denounced pornography.

The president is Archbishop Claudio Maria Celli. The secretary is Msgr. Paul Tighe. The undersecretary is Angelo Scelzo. Phone 06-6988-3197. E-mail *pccs@vatican.va*.

Prefecture of the Pontifical Household

The grand Apostolic Palace, where the pope resides, requires some looking after, and the Prefecture of the Pontifical Household does just that. In addition, the prefecture organizes papal audiences, both general ones and more private ones with heads of state and other important figures, and takes care of the pope's schedule both at home and outside Rome, in effect serving as a secretarial staff.

The prefect is an American, Archbishop James Michael Harvey. Phone 06-6988-3114.

Pontifical Commission *Ecclesia Dei*

Pope John Paul II founded this commission in 1988 to provide pastoral care to former followers of the late Archbishop Marcel Lefebvre. The French archbishop, who rejected the liturgical reforms and other aspects of the Second Vatican Council, was excommunicated after ordaining bishops without papal approval. The commission oversees matters related to the use among Catholics of the Tridentine Mass as revised in 1962, before the Vatican II liturgical reforms.

The president is Cardinal Dario Castrillon Hoyos. The secretary is Msgr. Camille Perl. Phone 06-6988-5213. E-mail *eccdei@ecclsdei.va*.

COVERING MAJOR VATICAN EVENTS

Conclave

If you cover the Vatican long enough, you'll probably get the chance to cover a conclave. This booklet will spare the details since you'll be flooded with information when the time comes, but here are the basics.

Foreign journalists generally invade Rome in the day or two following the death of a pope. The *Sala Stampa* processed more than 6,000 accreditation requests in the 10 days after Pope John Paul's death. Funeral rites are celebrated for nine consecutive days, called the *novendiales*, with burial between the fourth and sixth day after death. Before the funeral Mass, the pope's body lies in St. Peter's Basilica for viewing by the faithful.

The period in between popes is called an *interregnum*, during which time most Vatican business is suspended. In preparation for the coming conclave, cardinals gather for daily meetings called *general congregations*. The press office will release some information from the meetings, but most of the proceedings are confidential. That shouldn't stop you from trying to reach cardinals on your own; just don't be surprised if they don't answer your questions directly, and don't expect any specific prognostications as to so-called frontrunners. Keep in mind that while only cardinals under the age of 80 enter the conclave to vote, cardinals age 80 and above can still help shape the election by participating in the general congregations.

In the run-up to the conclave, Catholic News Service will carry biographical articles on cardinals who may be influential during the election. They're an indispensable resource, referencing biographical information; the curial, academic and diocesan positions cardinals have held; and some key issues they've spoken on or written about.

The conclave itself, when the world's cardinals gather in the Sistine Chapel to elect a new pope, is one of the Catholic Church's most fascinating rituals. But when they say secret they mean secret. Don't even hope for any leaks.

When the new pope emerges onto the balcony overlooking St. Peter's Square, he could be a known quantity, like Pope Benedict XVI was. As Cardinal Joseph Ratzinger, he had headed up the Congregation of the Doctrine of the Faith for 24 years, a high-profile position that garnered him a lot of press. Pope John Paul II, on the other hand, was relatively unknown to most of the world when he was elected.

Consistories

The word *consistory* comes from Latin, meaning "sitting together." In effect, it's a meeting, and other denominations also use the term. At the Vatican, it signifies a high-level meeting of cardinals. The most common type of consistory is an "ordinary" one, usually in which sainthood causes are formally resolved or new cardinals are created. The other, rarer type is called "extraordinary."

In the case of a consistory for new cardinals, the pope announces the names of those he's chosen to receive the "red hat" and the date of the consistory beforehand, perhaps a month or two in advance. If such a consistory brings you to Rome, it's probably because your hometown archbishop was named a cardinal, and you'll mainly focus on him. You'll want to find out as much of his personal schedule as you can, as well as the general schedule of the consistory and related Vatican events.

The consistory itself, when the pope officially creates, or invests, the new cardinals, usually takes place in St. Peter's Square. It is a Liturgy of the Word service, not a Mass, meaning there is no eucharistic celebration. During the consistory, each new cardinal kneels as the pope places a red, three-ridged hat called a *biretta* on his head. The phrase "getting the red hat" as a description of becoming a cardinal now refers to this moment, although historically it referred to the conferral of the *galero*, a broad-brimmed red hat with tassels hanging from each side, that popes gave cardinals from 1245 until Pope Paul VI suppressed the practice in 1969. In ecclesiastical heraldry cardinals may still use the galero with tassels over their coat of arms to symbolize their rank, but the pope no longer confers it when he makes a man a cardinal. While bishops may wear purple hats and robes, red is reserved to cardinals to represent their dedication to the church "*usque ad effusionem sanguinis*"—to the point of shedding their own blood.

Each new cardinal is assigned a "titular" church in Rome. While they obviously are not expected there on Sundays to celebrate Mass and preach, cardinals often pay a visit to their titular churches when they're in town. The titular churches make them titular clergy of Rome, hearkening back to an earlier time when the chief electors of a new pope were the clergy of Rome, the bishops of Rome's neighboring dioceses, and a few close advisors in the papal Curia. Eastern patriarchs in the College of Cardinals are not assigned a titular church in Rome; and since they do not normally wear Latin-style vestments, some Eastern-church leaders also may not receive a red biretta, or they may receive a red version of their own style of headdress.

The day after the consistory, the pope concelebrates Mass with the new cardinals, presenting each of them with a gold ring, another sign of their special communion with the church of Rome.

Ahead of the consistory itself, the pope may meet with the College of Cardinals and the cardinals-to-be in a closed-door assembly. Part of the meeting often focuses on a particular theme, with time set aside for less structured discussion. Check the *Bollettino* for whatever information the press office releases.

An ordinary public consistory in which sainthood causes are formally concluded typically involves only cardinals living in Rome. The meeting establishes the date of the canonization Mass, at which the pope officially declares the person a saint.

An extraordinary consistory involves all cardinals physically able to make the trip to Rome. The pope calls such a meeting as a consultative session on a specific topic. Among the six convened during Pope John Paul II's pontificate were a 1994 consistory on new religious movements and the defense of human life, and a 2001 assembly focusing on the church's priorities for the 21st century. The *Sala Stampa* will publish information in the *Bollettino* from an extraordinary consistory, which lasts three to four days, and certain cardinals may make their speeches available to reporters.

Synods

A synod is another type of meeting, in this case involving bishops, and is almost always held in two different instances: (1) a general session, or worldwide synod, which examines a specific theme concerning the entire church and gathers prelates from across the globe; or (2) a special session, which deals with a particular region, such as Africa. In either case, it is the pope who convokes one. Pope Paul VI reinstituted the synod structure following the Second Vatican Council.

Unlike an ecumenical council, which any bishop has a right to attend, synod participants are elected representatives of their bishops' conferences or are appointed by the pope. The Union of Superiors General, representing heads of male religious orders, also elects a small number of its members as synod participants. The synod may offer suggestions to the pope at the close of its assembly, but it does not enact any binding decisions.

In rare cases the pope will call an *extraordinary synod*, made up of the presidents of bishops' conferences and papal appointees. It's a smaller assembly, about half the size of a general or special session, either of which generally numbers about 250 participants. The last extraordinary synod was convened in 1985, to mark the 20th anniversary of Vatican II.

A preparatory document, called the *lineamenta*, goes out in advance to get comments. A follow-up document, the *instrumentum laboris*, outlines the topics. During the meeting itself, bishops present speeches more or less hewing to the chosen subjects. Pope Benedict XVI cut the amount of time per address down to six minutes, from his predecessor's limit of eight minutes. He also cut the length of synods themselves to three weeks, from the previous four. After the bishops' prepared remarks, the assembly holds an open discussion at the end of the day.

The press office will provide summaries of speeches and hold daily briefings—but, as with other Vatican meetings, don't expect an avalanche of information. The summaries and briefings tend to leave out the meat of the discussions. Some bishops may provide copies of their presentations.

Media coverage tends to focus on many of the same issues every time bishops gather: priestly celibacy, divorce, Catholic politicians, abortion, artificial contraception and other life issues. Be careful, however, not to conflate a couple of bishops' mentions of these topics with any kind of referendum, and don't ignore the other subjects at hand: liturgical translations, missionary work, social justice concerns, dwindling Christian populations in the Middle East, secular culture, and much, much more.

The final propositions that the synod delivers to the pope are secret but are often leaked to the press. At the close of the 2005 Synod on the Eucharist, Pope Benedict had them published.

The pope usually writes his own concluding document, called a *postsynodal apostolic exhortation*, several months later. During that time, a council made up of synod members serves as a follow-up group that helps the pope prepare the exhortation. A permanent Vatican synodal office organizes the assemblies.

Pallium

Another event that might have you crossing the Atlantic is the presentation of the pallium to your city's archbishop. Each year on the Solemnity of Sts. Peter and Paul (June 29), the pope places woolen bands called palliums around the necks of Latin rite archbishops whom he has appointed over the previous 12 months to be heads of metropolitan sees. Palliums are liturgical vestments that are worn over the chasuble at Mass.

Made from the wool of lambs blessed by the pope on Jan. 21, the feast of St. Agnes, the circular neckpieces are decorated with six black crosses, with two tails hanging in front and in back. The pallium represents the archbishop's authority over his ecclesiastical province and his unity with the pope, who also wears a pallium, and the wool recalls Jesus' words to Peter: "Feed my lambs" (Jn 21:15).

An archbishop may wear the pallium, in accord with liturgical norms, when celebrating Mass in any church in his ecclesiastical province, but he may not wear it at liturgical celebrations outside his province.

Saints

A canonization ceremony is a popular event for pilgrims and in certain cases can draw massive crowds, as with Padre Pio in 2002, when an estimated 300,000 thronged the Vatican.

The pope reads a decree proclaiming someone a saint during a Mass, often in St. Peter's Square but in many instances elsewhere in the world. The pope may preside at a canonization during a pastoral trip, as in 2007 in Sao Paulo, Brazil, where Pope Benedict XVI canonized Father Antonio Galvao, a Franciscan friar and the country's first native-born saint.

If you're interested in learning more about a saint-to-be and the long process of canonization, talk to his or her postulator, the person responsible for presenting and defending the evidence for a sainthood candidate. The church generally must confirm two miracles through the candidate's intercession before a declaration of sainthood. Most often the miracles involve someone's medically inexplicable cure from a disease or physical disorder. If they're still alive, those whose healings were officially deemed miraculous often attend the canonization ceremony and, as you might imagine, make for good interviews. Check, too, for pilgrims from the new saint's religious order, lay organization or city. For example, at Mother Theodore Guerin's 2006 canonization, students from a college in the Indiana town where she founded the Sisters of Providence traveled to Rome for the event.

Be careful to differentiate between saint, blessed and venerable. *Venerable* is the title used for someone whom the pope has decreed as having heroic virtues, the first step on the road to sainthood. *Blessed* is the title used for someone who has been beatified. Beatification requires the recognition of a miracle attributed to the candidate's intervention. Also note that the pope does not "make" or "create" someone a saint; he simply proclaims someone a *saint*.

In 2005 the Congregation for the Causes of Saints announced that Pope Benedict would preside only at canonizations, with a delegate handling beatifications—an earlier step in the process toward sainthood. His predecessor had presided at both ceremonies. The German pontiff, who as a cardinal had expressed concern over the number of causes being promoted, called for more scrutiny in choosing candidates for sainthood. During his 26-year tenure, Pope John Paul II canonized 482 people and beatified 1,341.

Click on "Saints & Blesseds" on the Vatican Web site's home page for a list of canonizations and beatifications during the pontificate of Pope John Paul, and to date under Pope Benedict.

RESOURCES

An easy way to keep track of the press office's communiqués is to subscribe online to VIS, the **Vatican Information Service**. On weekdays at about 3 p.m. Rome time, an e-mail goes out containing pontifical acts and nominations, a summary of the pope's homilies and speeches, presentations and communications concerning pontifical documents and Vatican departments, and official statements issued by the Holy See Press Office. It's sent out a few hours after the *Bollettino*, but in plenty of time to follow up on a story stateside.

To subscribe in English, go to *mlists.vatican.va/mailman/listinfo/visnews_en*.

Note that the VIS bulletins are only a rundown; the actual *Bollettini* may include additional information.

Keep an eye on **Vatican Radio** (*www.radiovaticana.org*) for noteworthy interviews with church officials. If you read Italian, the daily e-mail summary, including transcripts of the news program, can be informative. Send a request to *s-newsletter.rg14@vatiradio.va* if you want to subscribe. Otherwise, the English-language home page (*www.radiovaticana.org/en1/index.asp*) has a list of news and feature stories, though you'll need to download audio files for anything other than headlines. Also available on the Web site are general audiences, papal Masses and other Vatican events. If you're in Rome, tune to FM 93.3 or 105 to catch English news live at 8:30 a.m. and 6:15 p.m., and to FM 93.3 for the English feature program at 9:50 p.m. and again the next morning at 7 a.m. Both English news and feature broadcasts are also available on the Web site, and certain clips can be found as podcasts on iTunes.

The Vatican publishes a daily newspaper, *L'Osservatore Romano* (The Roman Observer). You'll recognize some information from the *Bollettini*, but more significant are the various scholarly articles that can serve as glosses on Vatican statements and church teaching. For example, the paper ran a piece in 2005 that further explained the Congregation for Catholic Education's instruction on accepting homosexuals as candidates for the priesthood. In 2006 a biology professor wrote an article on intelligent design, stating that the theory was not science. Unfortunately not all the articles are reprinted in the weekly English edition, which comes out on Wednesdays, and only a few of those are available on the Vatican's Web site at *www.vatican.va/news_ services/or/or_eng/index.html*. If you want the whole newspaper, you'll have to subscribe to the print edition. As with Vatican Radio, journalists can sign up online for a daily e-mail, which contains the entire newspaper, but the service is only available in Italian. For archival material and back issues, send an e-mail to *ornet@ossrom.va*.

Fides, the news agency of the Congregation for the Evangelization of Peoples, is another handy resource (*www.fides.org*). To receive the agency's news roundups via e-mail, send a request to *subscriptions@fides.org*. Because the congregation oversees missionary work, Fides focuses mainly on news outside the Vatican, but it does offer some good interviews with Vatican officials and others. Covering the Beijing Olympics? Get some background by reading comments from the bishop of Kaoshiung, Taiwan. Looking at Christians in the Middle East? Search for interviews with the Latin patriarch of Jerusalem.

La Civiltà Cattolica (Catholic Civilization) is an influential, biweekly Jesuit journal. While strictly speaking it's not a Vatican publication, articles are reviewed by the Vatican Secretariat of State before they go to press. English summaries of individual issues can be found at *www.laciviltacattolica.it*. To receive a newsletter via e-mail, send a request to *civcatt@laciviltacattolica. it*. The magazine often runs pieces on topical matters, such as church leaders intervening in public debate, the risks of virtual reality, and freedom of religion for Christians living in predominantly Muslim countries.

Catholic News Service, the Washington-based news agency of the U.S. Conference of Catholic Bishops, maintains a well-staffed bureau in Rome. For news from the Vatican, go to the home page (*www.catholicnews.com*) and click on the Vatican section. Most of the key stories are available on the Web site for free. It's a good idea to monitor the site daily, as CNS keeps abreast of all Vatican news, breaks down complex topics into easily understandable terms and provides good background on a host of church-related issues.

If you're in Rome, **pontifical universities** are great repositories of information. Run by the Jesuits, the Gregorian—or "the Greg," as it's affectionately known locally—and its associated Pontifical Biblical Institute can be particularly helpful (*www.unigre.it*). The Lateran (*www.pul.it*), Salesian (*www.unisal.it*), St. Thomas Aquinas (also called the Angelicum, *www.pust.urbe.it*), and Holy Cross Universities (*www.pusc.it*) are also good places to drum up sources. For an excellent specialized source on Islam, try the Pontifical Insitute for Arabic and Islamic Studies (*www.pisai.it*). More specifics are contained in the *Annuario.*

English-speaking seminaries, the North American College (NAC) first among them, can be effective resources as well. Keep them in mind for stories on vocations and clergy, and see if anyone from back home might be studying at the NAC.

For the Pontifical North American College (*www.pnac.org*), phone 06-684-931.

For the Venerable English College (*www.englishcollegerome.org*), phone 06-686-5808 or 8546.

For the Pontifical Irish College (*www.irishcollege.org*), phone 06-772-631.

For the Pontifical Scots College (*www.scotscollege.it*), phone 06-336-6801.

Almost all **religious orders** maintain a house in Rome, and for many that house is their main international headquarters. The bigger ones like the Jesuits, Franciscans, Dominicans, Benedictines and Paulists have press liaisons. They can be helpful, especially if back home a certain order is particularly prominent, or is tied to a specific parish you might be covering. The Web sites of religious orders vary greatly in media-friendliness, but you should be able to find basic contact information at any of them, even if the site does not have other information you're looking for.

Jesuits (*www.sjweb.info*): Phone 06-689-771.

Franciscans (*www.ofm.org*): Phone 06-6849-1366.

Dominicans (*www.op.org*): Phone 06-5794-0555.

Benedictine Confederation (*www.osb.org*): Phone 06-579-1319. For the Pontifical Athenaeum of Saint Anselm in Rome, run by the Benedictine order (*www.santanselmo.org*), phone 06-579-1410.

Paulist Fathers (*www.paulist.org*): Phone 06-488-2748. Santa Susanna (*www.santasusanna.org*), a Paulist-run church, is the national parish for American Catholics in Rome. Phone 06-4201-4554.

Covering the United States Conference of Catholic Bishops (USCCB)

The U.S. Conference of Catholic Bishops is a membership body composed of all the active Catholic bishops in the United States. Through it the bishops support and collaborate with one another in carrying out the church's mission, with a special emphasis on evangelization, or spreading the Gospel. While the bishops themselves are scattered across the country in their own dioceses, the national headquarters of the USCCB is at 3211 Fourth Street NE, Washington, DC 20017-1194.

Here is a brief overview of the staffing structure at USCCB headquarters. The main work of each department or secretariat will follow later, in the descriptions of the responsibilities of the committees they serve.

OFFICE OF THE GENERAL SECRETARY

The **general secretary of the USCCB** is Msgr. David Malloy. His office oversees the staff of about 250 priests, men and women religious, and laymen and laywomen who assist the bishops in their work. He is assisted by three associate general secretaries, an assistant general secretary for planning, and administrative staff.

The **associate general secretary for pastoral life** is Msgr. Ronny Jenkins. He handles canon law concerns and oversees eight conference secretariats:

- Clergy, Consecrated Life and Vocations.
- Cultural Diversity in the Church.
- Divine Worship.
- Doctrine.

- Ecumenical and Interreligious Affairs.
- Evangelization and Catechesis.
- Laity, Marriage, Family Life and Youth.
- Child and Youth Protection.

The **associate general secretary for policy and advocacy** is Nancy Wisdo. She oversees four departments or secretariats:

- Department of Justice, Peace and Human Development.
- Department of Migration and Refugee Services.
- Secretariat of Catholic Education.
- Secretariat of Pro-Life Activities.

The **secretary of communications** (not an associate general secretary) is Helen Osman. She oversees five offices:

- Office of Media Relations.
- Catholic News Service.
- USCCB Publishing.
- Office of Digital Media.
- Office of Film and Broadcasting (based in New York).

The **associate general secretary for administration** is Bruce Egnew. He oversees internal administrative and support services for the entire USCCB staff, such as accounting, business services, general services, human resources and information technology services. He also oversees the Office of National Collections, which coordinates several national collections taken up each year for church causes.

The **Office of the General Counsel** does not serve any particular programmatic committee of the bishops but is a source of legal advice to the entire conference and supports the work of diocesan attorneys, state Catholic conferences and other national, regional and local Catholic entities by providing advice on a variety of constitutional, tax, litigation and other matters.

CONTACTING THE USCCB

The USCCB Web site is ***www.usccb.org***. All media inquiries should be directed to the Office of Media Relations. Phone 202-541-3200.

For e-mail communications, the USCCB's general address format for all staff members is *<first initial plus last name>@usccb.org*. For example, the e-mail address of Sister Mary Ann Walsh, director of Media Relations, is *mwalsh@usccb.org*. One slight hitch: A few staff members use the first initial of their nickname instead of their formal name, and some have a first name that can be spelled more than one way. (E.g., is it a *C* for Catherine or *K* for Katherine? Is it a *T* for Tony or *A* for Anthony?) If in doubt send the e-mail to two or three variant addresses and find out which one goes through and which comes back undeliverable.

Technically Catholic News Service (CNS), a news agency formed by the U.S. bishops in 1920, is part of the USCCB, placed administratively under the conference's Office of the Secretary of Communications. But it is financially and editorially independent, and on the Web it has a separate domain. Its Web address is *www.catholicnews.com*. CNS officials and staff members can be reached by e-mail using the address format *<first initial plus last name>@catholicnews.com*.

USCCB MEETINGS

The highest authority in the USCCB is the general membership. It meets Monday through Thursday of the second full week of November in **general assembly** (in Washington for many years; in Baltimore since 2006). It also holds shorter general assemblies most years on a Thursday-through-Saturday in mid-June (changing in 2009 to a Wednesday-through-Friday). The spring assemblies are usually devoted more to discussion and reflection than to a business agenda. About every three to four years, the spring general assembly is replaced by a retreat-style **special assembly** for prayer and reflection, at which ordinarily no USCCB business is conducted. The spring meeting site varies from year to year.

Retreat-style special assemblies are closed to the media. General assemblies, spring or fall, are open to accredited media except for when the bishops meet in executive session or substitute prayer or reflection time for business sessions.

The basic agenda for USCCB general assemblies is determined about two months in advance by the next-highest authority in the conference, the USCCB Administrative Committee. Composed mainly of the conference officers (president, vice president, treasurer and secretary), chairmen of standing committees, and elected representatives of the 15 USCCB regions, the Administrative Committee meets just before the fall assembly and has at least two other business meetings each year, typically in March and September. These meetings are not open to media.

Retired bishops can voice their opinions but have no vote at USCCB general assemblies. They can serve on USCCB committees but cannot chair them. They cannot be conference officers. Auxiliary and coadjutor bishops have a vote in most matters, but only bishops who head dioceses can vote on national collections and issues of diocesan financial support for the USCCB. Auxiliaries and coadjutors can serve on committees and chair them and can be conference treasurer or secretary, but only diocesan bishops can hold the offices of president and vice president.

Bishops of the Latin rite and Eastern Catholic churches have a vote on statements and programs that affect the entire U.S. church, but the Eastern bishops do not vote on matters affecting only the Latin rite church—mainly liturgy and implementation or adaptation of the *Code of Canon Law* in the United States. (Each of the Eastern churches has its own liturgical norms and texts that are handled within their churches and not by the USCCB. In terms of church law, each of the Eastern churches has its own legislation within the general framework of the *Code of Canons of the Eastern Churches*—which, despite many similarities, is distinct from the Latin rite *Code of Canon Law*.)

While a simple majority of those present and voting at a meeting is all that is needed for elections and for many action items, on some matters the USCCB requires approval by at least two-thirds of all eligible voters. Pastoral letters and decisions on church law and liturgical matters are examples of items requiring such a two-thirds vote. Sometimes this means that a vote during the general assembly is inconclusive because there were not enough members present and voting. (Suppose, for example, there are 269 bishops eligible to vote on a question, but only 240 of them are at the meeting. The action needs 180 affirmative votes to pass or 90 negative votes to be defeated. If the vote is 175-65, the matter remains undecided until at least five of the 29 absent bishops vote for it or at least 25 vote against it.) In that case, those who did not vote at the time are polled by mail after the meeting. The final result usually is announced within a month after the meeting.

When the bishops vote on liturgical questions or other matters involving U.S. implementation of universal church norms or policies, the matter in question not only must be approved by two-thirds of the bishops, but must also be reviewed and confirmed by the Vatican. It is not unusual for such confirmation—technically called a *recognitio*, the Latin word for *recognition*—to take several months or even a year or two.

Under USCCB bylaws, any proposed action at a USCCB general assembly must be approved for placement on the agenda by the Administrative Committee. The documentation for that action item must then be sent to all bishops sufficiently in advance—generally interpreted as one month before the general assembly—to give them time to review it and submit amendments, modifications or other comments.

This is why, in a breaking political or diplomatic situation with moral or religious implications, it is not uncommon for the assembly to be asked to review a proposed statement by the USCCB president, suggest changes and later express support for the president's issuance of the statement. The parliamentary rule avoids a situation in which a need to address serious issues amid rapidly evolving circumstances might pressure bishops, without opportunity for due deliberation, into a conference statement that would have to stand the test of time for years or decades. The presidential statement alternative allows the bishops to address such issues and express a consensus but have their collective views articulated only by the authority of the conference president and not the entire body.

The USCCB Office of Media Relations will typically make the texts of a general assembly's proposed action items available to the media upon request within a few days after the bishops have had a chance to review the materials via the Internet, e-mail or postal mail. For example, if the fall meeting is Nov. 12-15, the materials will have been sent to the bishops by Oct. 12 and will typically be made available to media on request by Oct. 16 or so—allowing time first for those bishops who still receive hard copies of the documentation, instead of electronic versions, to receive the materials and review them.

The Office of Media Relations requires all journalists seeking to cover a bishops' meeting to apply in advance for credentials. The application form, which must be signed by a journalist's editor or other executive officer, is typically available online a month or so before the start of any meeting open to media coverage.

For those who have not requested advance copies of agenda documentation, at the start of each general assembly that documentation is available in the media center, along with media packets including the meeting agenda, press releases and other background materials. Reporters can pick up the documentation and all related materials when they register at the meeting site. Depending on the nature and extent of a meeting's documentation, the Office of Media Relations may also make it available on CD.

Because of space limitations in the meeting room, journalists working for outlets that only occasionally cover the bishops' meeting or for outlets of limited or infrequent circulation may be allowed access to the meeting room itself for only one or two sessions. The on-site media center, however, provides a live television feed of the entire proceedings, and all accredited journalists have access there throughout the meeting.

The bishops begin each morning and afternoon session with about 20 minutes of prayer based on the Liturgy of the Hours, the church's official daily prayer cycle that all Catholic bishops, priests and deacons are expected to observe to sanctify the entire day with devotion to God. Morning sessions end with the *Angelus*, the traditional noontime prayer of the church.

Usually there is a news conference after every major public session of a fall or spring meeting of the USCCB. All accredited journalists, photographers and TV camera crews have full access to such news conferences. The panelists at a news conference are typically the current chairman of the bishops' Committee on Communications and the chairmen of committees that have just presented or presided over discussion of action items at the preceding session of the meeting. When the news conference ends, journalists with additional questions often gather around one or another panelist to press for further clarifications.

Because a USCCB assembly is a business meeting, during business sessions news writers are restricted to tables assigned to the press gallery, and the access to the meeting floor for news photographers is limited. Generally photographers are allowed access for a limited time on the first morning of a meeting, provided they work from the peripheral areas of the meeting room, not up and down the aisles, where they would interfere with the conduct of the meeting itself. Television camera crews may record media conferences but generally must arrange with the sole television feed provider—EWTN in recent years—for TV footage of the meeting itself. EWTN is the Eternal Word Television Network, an independent Catholic TV cable network based in Irondale, Ala. Its Web address is *www.ewtn.com*.

During the course of a USCCB business meeting, any arrangements to interview bishops should be made through the USCCB Office of Media Relations, which always has a desk available at the meeting site to assist with such arrangements. It is best to check the meeting agenda and to ask for an interview to take place during a morning or afternoon coffee break, immediately after the closing of the morning or afternoon session, or immediately before the opening of the morning or afternoon session. Most bishops are reluctant to leave the room while a meeting is in session in order to give an interview, and other commitments may prevent many bishops from making time for an interview outside the coffee breaks or immediately before or after a business session. Anyone wishing to interview members of the USCCB staff may also use the interview desk to make such arrangements.

For **USCCB coverage throughout the year**, the latest news releases from the Office of Media Relations are available on the Web at *www.usccb.org*.

The USCCB Web site also features current documents and numerous background resources that journalists may find useful. Many of these can be accessed through departmental pages. For example, if you click "departments" and "ecumenical and interreligious affairs," you will find links to a comprehensive library of documents from the national and international ecumenical and interreligious dialogues in which the Catholic Church has engaged over the past 40-plus years. If you click "social development and world peace," you will find links to a similar library of statements by the U.S. bishops, USCCB testimony in Congress, and a variety of other resources on the bishops' positions on issues ranging from capital punishment to the war in Iraq, from the environment to AIDS, from the human dimensions of economic globalization to immigration, from human trafficking to health care, housing and minimum wage issues.

(A transitional note: In the spring of 2008, the Secretariat for Social Development and World Peace had been renamed the Department of Justice, Peace and Human Development, but most USCCB Web links had not caught up yet with the most recent structural name changes. Be prepared in 2008-2009 still to find old names or old-name links on the Web site for departments or programs that have been renamed.)

USCCB OFFICERS AND COMMITTEES

In its 2005-2007 reorganization, the USCCB reduced its number of committees significantly and committed itself to a more focused national policy and program agenda. The result has been far fewer committees and a major reduction in staffing at the USCCB national offices in Washington. By the time this booklet went to press, most but not all of the changes had taken effect. For that reason the following list is still somewhat provisional, but it reflects nearly all of the changes made in the reorganization.

The four **executive officers**—president, vice president, secretary and treasurer—serve three-year terms. In November 2007 Cardinal Francis E. George of Chicago was elected conference president, and Bishop Gerald F. Kicanas of Tucson, Ariz., was elected vice president. Since Bishop Kicanas was just entering his second year as USCCB secretary, there was a special election in which the bishops chose Bishop George V. Murry of Youngstown, Ohio, to fill the remaining two years of that term. Bishop Dennis M. Schnurr of Duluth, Minn., entered his final year as treasurer, and Archbishop Joseph E. Kurtz of Louisville, Ky., was elected treasurer-elect, to replace Bishop Schnurr the following November. By USCCB rules an officer cannot succeed himself in the same post; a lower officer may be elected to a higher office, but a higher officer may not be elected immediately to a lower office. Historically, in most presidential elections the outgoing vice president has been elected president.

For most news purposes, the most important committees of the USCCB are its programmatic committees (and related subcommittees). These follow alphabetically, with their relevant staff offices.

Committee on Canonical Affairs and Church Governance

This committee deals with adaptations of general church law to the U.S. context and with various other legal issues related to general church law as applied to the United States. Staff officer is Msgr. Ronny Jenkins, one of the associate general secretaries.

Committee on Catholic Education

The committee deals with public policy questions of vouchers, tuition credits or other tax breaks for families with children in private Catholic schools, and a variety of other issues related to Catholic elementary and secondary education throughout the diverse system of parish, diocesan and privately run Catholic schools. On internal church matters, it deals with standards for Catholic higher, secondary and elementary education in many areas. These range from the "*mandatum*" (episcopal authorization for Catholic theologians to teach in Catholic colleges and universities) to college campus ministry, from responsibilities of Catholic educators to the roles of Catholic schools in sexual education, from curriculum issues to bishops' responsibilities over the educational institutions in their dioceses.

The national staff serving the committee forms the USCCB Office of Catholic Education. The Office of Catholic Education works collaboratively with other USCCB secretariats and departments, as well as with national, state and local organizations that participate in the service of the Church's educational, catechetical and world missions ministries. The office's executive director is Marie A. Powell.

Committee on Clergy, Consecrated Life and Vocations

This committee is responsible for matters ranging from priestly life, deacons and ministry, to the religious life of men and women in religious orders, to programs encouraging the development of vocations to the ordained or religious life. It also handles bishops' relations with Catholics who are members of what the church calls *secular institutes*—Catholics who are not members of religious orders but who make special vows committing themselves to lives of poverty and chastity while making their living in the secular world in a variety of professions.

Msgr. Edward J. Burns is the executive director of the USCCB Secretariat of Clergy, Consecrated Life and Vocations.

Committee on Communications

The committee oversees the USCCB's media relations and publications and the church's engagement with film, broadcast, print and digital media. Helen Osman is the USCCB secretary of communications. Her Office of the Secretary of Communications oversees the following:

- The **Office of Media Relations**, through which the USCCB releases statements, makes official announcements and responds to inquiries from news media. Mercy Sister Mary Ann Walsh is its director.
- **USCCB Publishing**, which publishes texts of USCCB statements and pastoral letters, major papal and Vatican documents, and various other Catholic resources, such as catechetical and liturgical texts and educational and ministry resources. Its director is Paul Henderson.
- The **Office of Film and Broadcasting**, based in New York, which reviews movies, television programs and DVD releases both on their artistic merit and on their moral content and rates them for their suitability for viewing by various age groups. Harry Forbes is its director.
- The **Catholic Communication Campaign**, through which the bishops fund media programming, projects and resources that promote Gospel values and the pastoral teachings of the Catholic Church. A permanent subcommittee of the Committee on Communications oversees grant making, programming and relationships funded at the national level by the campaign, an annual national collection in Catholic parishes (half of which stays in the local diocese and half of which goes to national programs). Helen Osman is chief staff person for the subcommittee.
- **Catholic News Service**, a financially and editorially independent news agency established by the bishops in 1920 with print and broadcast subscribers—chiefly diocesan or national Catholic newspapers—in more than 40 countries. It also publishes *Origins*, the major English-language religious documentary service in the Catholic Church. Tony Spence is its director and editor in chief.

- The **Office of Digital Media**, which coordinates USCCB communications work in radio and television as well as on the Internet. Its director is Joseph Larson.

Committee on Cultural Diversity in the Church

Housing several formerly separate USCCB committees or subcommittees that dealt with pastoral ministry with specific racial, ethnic or other cultural groups, this committee has five permanent subcommittees: on African American Affairs, on Asian and Pacific Island Affairs, on Hispanic Affairs, on Native American Affairs, and on Pastoral Care of Migrants, Refugees and Travelers. Jesuit Father Allan Figueroa Deck is the executive director of the USCCB Secretariat of Cultural Diversity in the Church.

Committee on Divine Worship

Formerly called the Bishops' Committee on the Liturgy, it oversees translations of Latin liturgical texts and Scripture passages into English, Spanish and Native American languages (such as Navajo) for use in the United States; adaptation of liturgical norms and rites to U.S. use; development of original texts for some liturgies, such as the readings and proper prayers for Masses commemorating U.S. saints; and adaptation or implementation of Vatican norms for sacred art, architecture and music. In Catholic usage, *liturgy* refers not only to the Mass, but to all official forms of church worship. This includes the celebration of all the sacraments and the Liturgy of the Hours, which is the official prayers and readings all clergy and many religious are required to recite at various times daily to dedicate their entire day to God.

The executive director of the Secretariat of Divine Worship is Msgr. Anthony F. Sherman.

Committee on Doctrine

Charged with addressing doctrinal issues in a variety of contexts, this committee may be called upon to examine the orthodoxy of a U.S. Catholic theologian's teachings or writings, but more often it is asked to collaborate with other USCCB committees by assessing the doctrinal aspects of proposed statements, pastoral letters or policy positions. The Secretariat of Doctrine provides expertise on theological, moral and doctrinal matters, including issues of faith and science and Catholic health care. Capuchin Franciscan Father Thomas Weinandy is the secretariat's executive director.

Committee on Domestic Justice and Human Development

Formerly called the Committee on Domestic Policy, it seeks to spread knowledge and understanding of Catholic social teaching in the United States and to support and encourage programs in the church and in society that will advance human dignity and the common good. In the public policy arena, it advocates for the poor and vulnerable and for justice and peace. It has a permanent Subcommittee on the Catholic Campaign for Human Development, which oversees the program funding and education components of that yearly anti-poverty collection in U.S. parishes. Katherine Saile is director of domestic justice and human development.

Note: The Department of Justice, Peace and Human Development—formerly called the Department of Social Development and World Peace—coordinates the work of the USCCB's domestic and international offices and serves both this Committee on Domestic Justice and Human Development and the Committee on International Justice and Peace (see below). John Carr is secretary of justice, peace and human development. In the "About Us" link on its Web site, the department has a detailed list of staff members, their areas of responsibility, and their contact information.

Committee on Ecumenical and Interreligious Affairs

This committee oversees a wide range of U.S. and North American dialogues with other Christian denominations and with partners of other religious faiths. Ecumenical dialogue partners include the Orthodox, Eastern Orthodox, Anglican (Episcopalian), Lutheran, Reformed, Presbyterian, Methodist and various other churches. In interreligious dialogue the committee has consultations with several U.S. Jewish organizations, three regional Muslim groups, Buddhists, Sikhs and other religions. Because of the religious diversity of the United States and its long history of religious tolerance and dialogue, many of the U.S. Catholic dialogues with other Christian faiths and with non-Christian religious groups have set a standard for such dialogues around the world.

Father James Massa is executive director of the USCCB Secretariat of Ecumenical and Interreligious Affairs.

Committee on Evangelization and Catechesis

This committee, which collaborates closely with the Committee on Catholic Education, oversees the bishops' evangelization activities and practices related to the Rite of Christian Initiation of Adults (RCIA—the church's basic program for admitting adult converts to Catholicism), the *Catechism of the Catholic Church* and other catechetical activities. Its Subcommittee on the Use of the Catechism reviews Catholic school and parish-based religious education texts for adequacy and accuracy in presenting Christian beliefs and church teachings at various ages.

The Secretariat of Evangelization and Catechesis, in collaboration with the Office of Catholic Education, works to ensure that Catholic efforts to spread the Gospel and teach the Catholic faith are effective, orthodox and pastorally sound. Msgr. Daniel Kutys is executive director of the secretariat.

Committee on International Justice and Peace

Formerly called the Committee on International Policy, it seeks to implement Catholic teachings on peace and justice in the international field. It collaborates with the Holy See and bishops' conferences around the world to call attention to situations of injustice and violations of human rights and dignity, to promote human solidarity and to advocate for U.S. policies that will contribute to a more just and peaceful world and for sustainable development among the world's poor and vulnerable populations. The director of international justice and peace is Stephen Colecchi.

Note: The Department of Justice, Peace and Human Development—formerly called the Department of Social Development and World Peace—coordinates the work of the USCCB's domestic and international offices and serves both the Committee on Domestic Justice and Human Development (see above) and this Committee on International Justice and Peace. John Carr is secretary of justice, peace and human development. In the "About Us" link on its Web site, the department has a detailed list of staff members, their areas of responsibility, and their contact information.

Committee on Laity, Marriage, Family Life and Youth

This committee oversees efforts by the bishops to promote marriage and family life, promote the development of youth and young adults in the church, and articulate the role of laypeople in the life and mission of the church—including bringing their faith into the workplace, politics and other areas of civil society. It also works to understand and advance the place of lay ecclesial ministry in church life. The committee was formed by merging three former committees—on the laity, on marriage and family, and on women in society and the church. The former Committee on the Laity had subcommittees on lay ministry and on youth and young adults, and the new committee includes the responsibilities of those former subcommittees as well. The executive secretary of the Secretariat of Laity, Marriage, Family Life and Youth is H. Richard McCord.

Committee on Migration

This committee advocates more just and humane U.S. immigration policies and works with and on behalf of immigrants, refugees and asylum seekers in the United States, resettling them and providing them with a wide range of social, educational, financial and other services. The Department of Migration and Refugee Services, often simply referred to as MRS, is the USCCB staff agency overseen by the committee. Through its network of diocesan agencies, MRS has resettled more than 800,000 refugees since 1975, making it the largest U.S. agency in that field. Its director is Ambassador Johnny Young, formerly of the U.S. State Department.

Committee on National Collections

This committee oversees the promotion and fund raising, but not grant making, of three annual national collections held in U.S. Catholic dioceses and parishes: the Catholic Communication Campaign, The Catholic Relief Services (CRS) Collection, and the Catholic Campaign for Human Development.

It also oversees the promotion, the fund raising and, through permanent subcommittees, the grant making of three other national collections: Home Missions, the Church in Latin America, and Aid to the Church in Central and Eastern Europe.

It oversees the promotional work for Peter's Pence, an annual collection given to the pope for charitable use at his discretion, and it tracks the amount raised, although the dioceses give the proceeds to the pope, directly or through his apostolic nuncio in Washington.

The executive director of the Office of National Collections is Patrick Markey.

The committee also has a temporary subcommittee on the church in Africa, for which the bishops have been seeking to provide some form of ongoing, coordinated assistance from the U.S. church, but without the benefit of a yearly collection in all U.S. parishes.

Grant making for the CCHD collection is overseen by a subcommittee of the Committee on Domestic Justice and Human Development. A subcommittee of the Committee on Communications oversees use of Catholic Communication Campaign funds. The Administrative Committee oversees the distribution of The CRS Collection.

Committee on Pro-Life Activities

This committee seeks to raise U.S. awareness of the dignity and sacredness of human life from conception to natural death and to promote policies and practices supportive of human life and dignity. It seeks to advance American society's support for laws prohibiting or restricting abortion, euthanasia, human cloning and embryonic stem cell research involving the destruction of human embryos. It sponsors Respect Life Month each October to advocate for comprehensive respect for human life and dignity, including advocacy for the poor, elderly and other vulnerable members of society as well as the unborn who find their basic rights at risk. The executive director of the Office of Pro-Life Activities is Tom Grenchik.

Committee on the Protection of Children and Young People

This committee seeks to ensure that dioceses meet high standards in their policies, programs and actions to prevent sexual abuse of minors by clergy, other church workers or volunteers and that dioceses respond effectively to allegations of such abuse through assistance to victims, thorough investigation of allegations, cooperation with civil authorities, and removal from ministry of those who have committed such crimes. It oversees implementation of the *Charter for the Protection of Children and Young People* adopted by the bishops in June 2002 and of the "essential norms" adopted by the bishops with Vatican approval as special U.S. church legislation for handling all allegations of child sexual abuse by any deacon or priest. The committee also has responsibility for overseeing the two most extensive studies of child sexual abuse ever conducted anywhere—one (completed in 2004) on the nature and extent of Catholic clergy sexual abuse of minors in the United States from 1950 to 2002, and one (still underway in 2008) on the causes and context of that abuse.

The Secretariat of Child and Youth Protection staffs the committee. Its executive director is Teresa Kettelkamp. The secretariat also provides staff assistance to the National Review Board, a board appointed by the USCCB president to review diocesan compliance with the child protection charter; to oversee annual diocesan audits on child protection policies, procedures and practices; and to recommend ways that abuse prevention and child protection may be enhanced in the future.

OTHER USCCB COMMITTEES

In addition to the programmatic committees, the USCCB has the Administrative Committee, Committee on Budget and Finance, Committee on Priorities and Plans, and Executive Committee.

Administrative Committee

Briefly described earlier in this chapter, the Administrative Committee is the highest authority of the conference after the entire body of bishops when they meet in general assembly. For legal purposes it also serves as the Board of Trustees of the USCCB as a civil corporation. In addition to the four conference officers, its members include the chairmen of all the standing committees who are elected by the general membership, as well as an elected representative from each of the 15 USCCB regions. (One region, created in 2006, consists of all the bishops of the Eastern Catholic churches. The other 14 are geographic regions of the bishops of the Latin Church.) Also on the Administrative Committee are the chairman of the Board of Directors of Catholic Relief Services, if he is not the USCCB president, and the immediate past president of the USCCB during the first year after completion of his term. Each region also elects an alternate, who may cast his vote at any meeting not attended by the region's representative.

Administrative Committee meetings are closed to the public and the media, but any bishop may attend. In practice, few bishops who are not Administrative Committee members attend those meetings unless they have a special interest in or responsibility for a particular item on the agenda. For example, a bishop heading a subcommittee or task force that has an action item before the Administrative Committee might attend as a resource or advocate for that item, even though he is not on the Administrative Committee.

The Administrative Committee's work is mainly internal to the work of the conference. For example, it oversees the work of the USCCB General Secretariat, reviews and approves the agenda for each general assembly, makes recommendations on proposals for that assembly, reviews actions of the Executive Committee, and manages USCCB corporate affairs and property.

Its main public activity consists of occasionally issuing statements, reflecting policy positions previously adopted by the full body of bishops, on urgent new public developments or other matters between meetings of the general assembly. For example, for decades before 2007, the quadrennial USCCB statement to U.S. Catholics on political responsibility (more recently described as "faithful citizenship") during the year before presidential elections was issued by the Administrative Committee. It addressed a variety of public policy issues then current in the approaching national elections and reflected relevant statements the bishops had made in recent years on those issues, such as abortion, agriculture, capital punishment, crime, defense spending, employment, environment, family life, foreign aid, health care, housing, immigration, minimum wage, peace, poverty, urban renewal, and war and peace. In 2007 the bishops promoted their faithful citizenship statement from an Administrative Committee statement to one issued by the entire body of bishops.

Msgr. David Malloy, USCCB general secretary, is the chief staff officer for the Administrative Committee.

Executive Committee

Composed of the four conference officers (president, vice president, treasurer and secretary) and one Administrative Committee member elected by that committee, the Executive Committee can be convened at any time by the USCCB president to "carry on urgent business of the conference between meetings of the Administrative Committee or the plenary assembly," to oversee staff personnel matters, or to make recommendations to the president or to committee chairmen about USCCB business. At the public level, it rarely issues a statement on its own; most of its work is internal and rarely of direct media interest. Msgr. Malloy is chief staff officer.

Committee on Priorities and Plans

For news purposes, this committee too is basically an inside-the-beltway committee whose decisions and proposals rarely reach the level of general news interest. It helps the bishops establish goals, objectives and five-year planning cycles for conference activities and priorities; coordinates the development of specific initiatives for priority issues; approves proposals of annual plans related to those goals, objectives and initiatives for presentation to the U.S. bishops; and on an ongoing basis monitors how all those things are being implemented. It also oversees the annual job of nominating bishops for committee chairmanships and conference office posts. The USCCB secretary is automatically chairman of this committee. Msgr. Malloy is its chief staff officer.

Committee on Budget and Finance

Another inside-the-beltway committee for most news purposes, this committee reviews all USCCB budget and financial management operations and develops budget proposals to align budget and operations with conference priorities and strategic plans.

The USCCB treasurer is automatically chairman of this committee. It has an Audit Subcommittee that oversees USCCB financial audits, conflict of interest policies and other policies and practices regarding the ethics and integrity of overall USCCB management and business practices. Msgr. Malloy is chief staff officer of the committee.

MAJOR CATHOLIC ORGANIZATIONS OR AGENCIES

The U.S. Catholic Church has almost innumerable official and unofficial Catholic organizations and agencies that act on behalf of the church or represent it or its members, unofficially or in varying degrees of official capacity. Here is a list of some of the main officially recognized organizations and agencies directly connected to or recognized by the Holy See or the U.S. bishops, with brief descriptions and contact references.

Heads of Religious Orders

Conference of Major Superiors of Men (CMSM)

Canonically recognized by the Vatican as the U.S. representative agency for provincials or other major superiors of men's religious orders in the United States, CMSM coordinates their activities on public policy and justice and peace issues and speaks on their behalf on a variety of issues in the U.S. church and civil society. Its headquarters are in Silver Spring, Md. The phone number is 301-588-4030. The Web site is *www.cmsm.org*.

Leadership Conference of Women Religious (LCWR)

LCWR is the first representative agency of U.S. provincials or other major superiors of women's religious orders recognized by the Vatican. Its members lead about 67,000 sisters in 370 orders or congregations, representing about 90 percent of the nuns in the United States. Its headquarters are in Silver Spring, Md. The phone number is 301-588-4955. The Web site is *www.lcwr.org*.

Council of Major Superiors of Women Religious (CMSWR)

Formed in 1992 by major superiors of women religious not affiliated with LCWR, CMSWR is also recognized by the Vatican as a representative agency of provincials or other major superiors of women's religious orders. About 10 percent of U.S. women religious belong to orders or congregations whose leaders belong to the CMSWR. Its headquarters are in Washington. The phone number is 202-832-2575. The Web site is *www.cmswr.org*.

Vatican or Vatican-Related Organizations and Agencies

Apostolic Nunciature

Since 1984 the Holy See and the United States have had full diplomatic relations. The Vatican ambassador to the United States is called the *apostolic nuncio* or *papal nuncio*, and the Vatican Embassy in Washington is also called the *apostolic nunciature*. The nuncio is Archbishop Pietro Sambi.

In addition to his diplomatic functions with the U.S. government, the nuncio serves as the chief liaison of the pope and Vatican offices to the U.S. church. Before diplomatic relations were established, the papal representative in the United States was called an *apostolic delegate*, his residence and offices were called the *apostolic delegation*, and Vatican relations with the U.S. church were his primary function.

The nuncio usually announces new episcopal appointments in the United States at the same time that they are announced in Rome, and he often attends episcopal ordinations as the pope's representative.

The nuncio also serves as the Vatican's permanent observer to the Washington-based Organization of American States.

The nunciature's phone number is 202-333-7121.

Permanent Observer Mission of the Holy See to the United Nations

Although the Holy See is not a member state of the United Nations, since 1964 it has had a Permanent Observer Mission to the United Nations in New York. In 2004 the UN General Assembly passed a resolution by acclamation strengthening the mission's status. The Holy See now enjoys, among other things, the right to participate in the general debate of the General Assembly, the right of reply, the right to have its communications issued and circulated directly as official documents of the assembly, and the right to co-sponsor draft resolutions and decisions that make reference to the Holy See. In December 2006 Congress authorized the president to grant members of the observer mission the same diplomatic immunity and privileges that the United States, as host country, grants to UN ambassadors and their staffs.

Archbishop Celestino Migliore is apostolic nuncio and permanent observer of the Holy See to the United Nations. The mission's main phone number is 212-370-7885. Its Web site is *www.holyseemission.org*.

Catholic Near East Welfare Association (CNEWA)

Based in New York, CNEWA is a special agency of the Holy See, established in the United States by Pope Pius XI in 1926 out of his concern for the post-World War I humanitarian and religious needs in Russia and the Near East. It supports the pastoral mission of the Eastern Catholic churches—the needs of the churches, institutions and persons under the jurisdiction of the Vatican's Congregation for Eastern Churches and the Permanent Interdicasterial Commission for the Church in Eastern Europe—and provides humanitarian assistance to the needy and afflicted without regard to nationality or creed. It seeks to promote Catholic-Orthodox unity and raises and distributes funds to help meet the material and spiritual needs of the people it serves.

In 1949 Pope Pius XII formed the **Pontifical Mission for Palestine**, under the direction of the general secretary of CNEWA, to help meet the social and humanitarian needs of Palestinian refugees from the Arab-Israeli conflict following the establishment of the Israeli state in 1948. Since then CNEWA's presence in the Middle East under the pontifical mission's umbrella has expanded significantly. Religion-related conflicts in Lebanon, Ethiopia and other countries in the Middle East and North Africa, most recently Iraq, have drawn CNEWA's attention to relief and rebuilding in those nations as well.

In the establishment of both CNEWA and the Pontifical Mission for Palestine, the Vatican relied on the postwar economic capabilities of American Catholics, after two world wars when most of Europe was in economic shambles, to supply much-needed aid in those areas of Eastern Europe and the Middle East where Christianity faced major challenges, and where the people of those regions, whatever their faith, faced immense religious, political, social, economic, educational, health and other challenges.

CNEWA's basic mission is to work on behalf of the Christian East in those lands in which, from ancient times, the majority of Christians are members of the various Eastern churches. In its 80-year evolution, its mandate has grown to encompass the churches and peoples of the Middle East, Northeast Africa, India, and Eastern Europe, as well as Eastern Catholics throughout the world.

It assists projects and programs of pastoral support, humanitarian assistance, interfaith communication and public awareness in all those areas.

In recent years leaders of the Catholic Church in Canada and in other countries where the hierarchy has had special concerns about or programs for the church and society in the Near East and Middle East have begun to develop ways to coordinate their concerns and activities with CNEWA and the Pontifical Mission for Palestine. As a result, a new national branch, CNEWA Canada, has been formed, and bishops in Latin America, Australia, Austria, Germany and Switzerland have begun to study the possibility of developing other national or regional offices of CNEWA.

The archbishop of New York is ex officio president and director of CNEWA. The secretary general and chief executive officer, nominated by the New York archbishop and elected by its trustees, is Msgr. Robert L. Stern. The associate general secretary is Maronite Catholic Chorbishop John D. Faris. The main phone number is 212-826-1480. The Web site is *www.cnewa.org*.

Pontifical Mission Societies

The Vatican Congregation for the Evangelization of Peoples—which oversees church activities in those parts of the world where the church is not yet sufficiently established to support itself economically or in terms of priestly and religious vocations and other organizational infrastructures—provides a network of spiritual and financial support for the missions through its four pontifical mission societies, which have national and diocesan branches around the world.

The **Society for the Propagation of the Faith** is the largest of the four. It provides support to mission dioceses in Africa, Asia, the Pacific islands and remote areas of Latin America. The **Holy Childhood Association** seeks to make children aware of the church's missionary activities and help them develop a missionary spirit themselves by contributing to programs directed at aiding children in mission countries. The **Society of St. Peter the Apostle** directs its funding efforts toward support of seminaries and seminarians in mission lands. The fourth society, the **Missionary Union of Priests and Religious**, is not a fund-raising group but focuses on the spiritual aspect, what is often called *mission animation*. It seeks to educate and inspire priests, men and women religious, pastoral leaders and religious educators so that they may better animate others to share their faith, supporting the church's missionary work and perhaps even becoming missionaries themselves.

All four societies have their U.S. national offices in New York. They share a single national director, Msgr. John E. Kozar. The phone number is 212-563-8700. The Web site is *www.worldmissions-catholicchurch.org*.

Other National Organizations

Catholic Charities USA

Founded in 1910 as the National Conference of Catholic Charities, Catholic Charities USA is a network of more than 1,700 Catholic Charities agencies and other member institutions nationwide, many of them sponsored by local dioceses, that assist more than 7.8 million people of all faiths every year. Taken together, those agencies and institutions form the largest private-sector non-profit provider of charitable and social services in the United States.

Catholic Charities USA provides leadership and support to enhance the work of the local agencies in their efforts to reduce poverty, support families and empower communities. It also serves as a national voice for the Catholic Charities agencies and their clients, promoting their work, articulating the Catholic values underlying their commitment to those in need, and advocating federal legislation and policies that will better meet the needs of the poor and vulnerable.

Since 1990 Catholic Charities USA has also had a Disaster Response Office to bring national relief to people suffering losses from hurricanes, tornadoes, floods or other disasters. Channeling funds through local Catholic Charities partners, this aid ranges from immediate assistance like food, shelter and crisis counseling to intermediate and long-term assistance to restore and rebuild communities and families over months and years following the disaster.

Catholic Charities USA has headquarters in Alexandria, Va. Its president is Father Larry Snyder. The phone number of the manager of media relations, Shelley Borysiewicz, is 703-236-6218. The Web site is *www.catholiccharitiesusa.org*.

Catholic Relief Services (CRS)

Formed by the U.S. bishops in 1943 to serve World War II survivors in Europe, CRS is the official international relief and development agency of the U.S. Catholic community. With a staff of 5,000 around the globe, it serves more than 80 million impoverished and disadvantaged people in more than 100 countries. It serves people based solely on need, regardless of their race, religion or ethnicity, following the Gospel call to work for charity and justice by alleviating suffering and aiding in the development of people. Its program areas include emergency relief, HIV and AIDS, health, agriculture, education and peace building.

The CRS board of directors is chaired by a bishop, and the majority of its members are bishops. The president is Ken Hackett. The headquarters is in Baltimore, Md. Its Internet site, *crs.org*, includes contact information for communications personnel in Baltimore and for regional information directors around the world. The phone number for Elizabeth Griffin, director of communications, is 410-951-7361.

National Religious Retirement Office (NRRO)

With offices at the USCCB headquarters, NRRO assists religious communities that face an aging membership without enough funds to meet their rapidly rising living and health care costs. In a 2006 report the office said that three years earlier, according to an actuarial study, U.S. religious orders had a gap of $8.7 billion between their retirement investments and their retirement liabilities, and that the gap would grow to about $20 billion by 2023 if nothing was done.

Besides direct financial grants, the office's services include helping orders to develop and administer retirement plans and make the best use of their resources. Grants come from a national collection for the needs of aging religious that raises about $30 million a year. Sponsored jointly by the USCCB, CMSM, LCWR and CMSWR, the retirement office oversees the collection and distribution of the funds. Precious Blood Sister Janice B. Bader is director of the office. The phone number is 202-541-3215. The Web site is *www.usccb.org/nrro*.

Catholic Legal Immigration Network, Inc. (CLINIC)

Formed by the USCCB in 1988 as a legally distinct subsidiary, CLINIC is a nonprofit public interest legal corporation that supports a network of community-based immigration programs. It has coordinated some of the largest programs in the nation for asylum, detained immigrants, immigration appeals and naturalization. Its network of more than 150 diocesan and other affiliated immigration programs, with more than 250 field offices in 48 states, employs about 1,200 attorneys and paralegals who assist 400,000 low-income immigrants a year on legal matters. The executive director is Donald M. Kerwin. The Web site is *www.cliniclegal.org*. Melissa Williams is media relations coordinator: phone 202-635-5810 or e-mail *mwilliams@cliniclegal.org*.

Covering the Local Church

The Second Vatican Council described the local or particular church as a "community existing around an altar, under the sacred ministry of the bishop" (*Lumen Gentium*, no. 26). The universal (catholic) church is a communion of all those particular churches. In other words, the archdiocese or diocese, as a local community of Christ's followers led and served by a bishop with the assistance of his priests, is one of the core realities in the Catholic understanding of what it means to be a church.

For those not familiar with the intricacies of how the Catholic Church operates at the diocesan or parish level, this chapter is intended to be a brief roadmap to the most salient parts of that structure. See the Glossary in this book for a definition or description of many of the terms you may run across here.

DIOCESES AND ARCHDIOCESES

In their internal operation, dioceses and archdioceses are virtually alike. But an archbishop, head of an archdiocese, has additional responsibilities because he is also head of an ecclesiastical province. The province comprises the archdiocese and the dioceses under it. In a province, the archdiocese is referred to as the *metropolitan see* and the dioceses are *suffragan sees*.

The diocese is headed by a bishop or, when one bishop has died or retired and his successor has not yet been installed, by an administrator. Theologically, for Catholics the bishop is a successor of the first apostles, the chief teacher and guardian of faith and morals for the people entrusted to him. He has the duty of ministering to his people, leading them to holiness by his own example, by teaching and preaching, and by administering the sacraments.

Central Offices

The central offices of a diocese—called by a variety of names such as *chancery*, *Catholic center*, *pastoral center*—are usually located in the *see city*, the city after which the diocese is named. But there are exceptions. For example, the Archdiocese of Santa Fe's Catholic center is located in Albuquerque, N.M.; the chancery office of the Diocese of Baker, Ore., is located in Bend.

The way diocesan offices are structured varies widely from one diocese to the next. But there are some offices every diocese must have by church law, such that vicar general, chancellor, finance office and a tribunal; and there are some offices that virtually every diocese needs as a practical matter, such as offices for Catholic schools, religious education or catechetics, Catholic Charities or social services, and liturgy or worship.

Bishop

The bishop who heads a diocese is called the *diocesan bishop*. He is the chief legislator, executive and judge in the diocese. He alone can legislate. He can exercise executive power personally or through vicars general or episcopal vicars. He can exercise judicial power personally or through a judicial vicar and judges.

If the diocesan bishop has other bishops assisting him, they are called *auxiliary bishops*. In some circumstances, especially if he has health problems that limit his ministry or if he is nearing retirement, a diocesan bishop may ask for a coadjutor. A *coadjutor bishop* has right of succession; that is, upon the death or retirement of the diocesan bishop, the coadjutor immediately becomes the new diocesan bishop. Auxiliary bishops do not have the right of succession.

Auxiliary bishops always have the title of bishop—*Auxiliary Bishop John Smith, Bishop Smith*—whether they serve in a diocese or archdiocese. When a coadjutor is appointed to an archdiocese, however, he has the title of archbishop: *Coadjutor Archbishop John Smith, Archbishop Smith*.

Vicar General and Episcopal Vicars

The bishop's chief administrative aide, the *vicar general* must be a priest or bishop, ordinarily with a licentiate or doctorate in canon law or theology. Small dioceses typically have only one, but larger dioceses may have several. A vicar general has the same ordinary executive powers over the whole diocese as the diocesan bishop, with the exception of those powers the bishop has reserved to himself and those reserved to the bishop alone by church law.

Ordinarily the priest or bishop designated as moderator of the curia is also a vicar general. If there is a coadjutor bishop, church law says he is to be made a vicar general. If there is an auxiliary bishop, he is to be made a vicar general.

If there are several auxiliaries, as there typically are in very large dioceses or archdioceses like Chicago, New York or Los Angeles, those auxiliaries not designated as vicars general are to be made *episcopal vicars*. Priests may also be named episcopal vicars. Within the geographic area or type of affairs entrusted to him, an episcopal vicar has the same executive powers that a vicar general has over the whole diocese. Often episcopal vicars are responsible for a particular geographic region of the diocese.

Chancellor

The chancellor is the official keeper of the diocesan records and archives and is the diocesan notary. He or she is responsible for recording all official diocesan actions and overseeing parish record keeping. Once only priests could be chancellors, but under the new *Code of Canon Law* adopted in 1983, ordination is no longer a prerequisite. Since then a number of women have become chancellors in U.S. dioceses; it is the highest-ranking diocesan position open to women.

Judicial Vicar and Tribunal Officials

Although the diocesan bishop is the chief local ecclesiastical judge in church law, he can and ordinarily does delegate that responsibility to a *judicial vicar* and to judges who sit on the diocesan *tribunal*, or court. The judicial vicar oversees the activities of the court and is one of its judges. Most court cases in a diocese concern petitions by civilly divorced Catholics to have their former marriage declared null—commonly called an *annulment*.

Sometimes the diocesan courts are referred to as *marriage tribunals*. This term is technically inaccurate since they do have jurisdiction over other cases as well, but it is fairly accurate as an empirical description of what most of these courts actually do most of the time.

The judicial vicar must be a priest. Although some other judges on the tribunal need not be ordained, on any three-judge panel (the normal number to hear any case) at least two must be priests. Apart from judges, other key tribunal officials include the *defender of the bond*—in essence the church attorney charged with advocating for the validity of a marriage against any claim that it was not valid—and the advocate for the person claiming a previous marriage was null. Judges must have graduate degrees in canon law.

Other Vicars

"Vicar"—from a Latin word for "substitute"—is used in a variety of contexts in the Catholic Church, mainly to refer to officials who can substitute for a bishop in his various duties. In addition to the vicars general, episcopal vicars and judicial vicars mentioned above, "vicar" can be used for various officials in diocesan offices who are charged with overseeing a particular region or ministry or other function on behalf of the bishop. Examples are vicar for priests, vicar for religious, vicar for Spanish-speaking Catholics, regional vicar, vicar for ethnic ministries. In each case, the person holding the title acts as the bishop's chief representative in a particular region of the diocese, particular area of ministry, or oversight over ministries. Some dioceses divide their geographic regions as *vicariates*, assigning a vicar to head each one.

Financial Officer and Council

A bishop is required to have a financial officer and financial council. For diocesan financial transactions exceeding a certain amount, he must consult with the council; at a higher threshold, he must have the council's consent; at a still higher threshold, he must obtain consent from the Vatican. These figures have come into prominent news play several times in recent years in bankruptcy protection dealings by several U.S. dioceses to settle lawsuits over the sexual abuse of minors by clergy, including a notable case in which the Boston archdiocesan financial council rejected a proposed settlement that required its approval. The dollar amounts for each threshold have been set by the USCCB with confirmation by the Vatican, but over the years they have changed.

Other Typical Diocesan Offices

Most dioceses will also have offices for some or all of the following:

- Catholic Charities and/or social services.
- Catholic schools.
- Religious education.
- Evangelization.
- Liturgy or worship.
- Communications.
- Pro-life activities.
- Ecumenical and interreligious relations.

Presbyteral Council and College of Consultors

Each diocese has a *priests' council*—called a *presbyteral council* in church law—which serves as a consultative body to the bishop. About half the priests on the council are elected by their fellow priests. In addition, some priests, such as certain diocesan officials, may belong to the council automatically, and some may be appointed by the bishop. The statutes of the council determine whether or to what extent priests in religious orders residing in the diocese are also represented. From among the members of the priests' council the bishop selects six to 12 priests to serve as the diocesan *college of consultors*. When the diocesan bishop dies, retires or is transferred, if there is no auxiliary bishop, the college of consultors is responsible for the governance of the diocese and elects a diocesan administrator from among the priests of the diocese. On certain matters the administrator must consult with the college. The priests' council is automatically dissolved when a diocese is vacant, but the college of consultors is not.

Pastoral Council

A consultative body to the bishop, a diocesan *pastoral council* is made up mainly of laypeople but typically includes representatives of the diocese's clergy and religious as well. Church law says it is to be convened at least once a year. It is automatically dissolved when the diocese is vacant.

Local Diocesan Directory

Most dioceses produce an annual directory of their diocesan offices and all parishes, including staff personnel at the diocesan and parish level. A number of dioceses have this information on an Internet site, but Internet savvy varies widely from diocese to diocese. If you are new to covering religion, contact your diocesan communications officer to find out what directory resources the diocese has online or in print to help you do your job.

PARISHES

The priest who heads a parish is its *pastor* and is appointed by the diocesan bishop. Sometimes between pastors a parish may be headed temporarily by an administrator, also appointed by the bishop. In dioceses where there are insufficient priests to have a resident pastor in every parish, some parishes may be administered by a deacon, sister, brother or layperson. In such cases a priest who resides elsewhere must be named the *canonical pastor*. The canonical pastor ordinarily provides sacramental ministry to the community. If someone who is not a priest is appointed to coordinate other parish activities, he or she may be in charge of a wide range of things such as adult and child religious education and formation, sacramental preparation, coordination of music ministry and other liturgical ministries, oversight of social and other outreach ministries, and worship services such as the Liturgy of the Hours or a Liturgy of the Word on weekdays or on Sunday when there is no priest available to celebrate Mass.

Parishes without resident priests have become more common in recent years in town-and-country America, especially rural or semi-rural dioceses in the Middle West and Upper Midwest, where previously there were many parishes with only one priest and where now a lack of priests leads to parishes being served sacramentally by a nonresident priest.

On the opposite end of the parish spectrum are many urban, suburban and exurban parishes—especially in the East and in larger metropolitan areas across the country—where parish size and diversity has led to multiple ministries, many led by lay ecclesial ministers. Those parishes may include priests who are *associate pastors*, also sometimes called *parochial vicars*. They may also have lay pastoral associates, religious education coordinators, parochial elementary or high school principals, teachers, youth ministers, liturgy coordinators, music coordinators, office managers and a variety of other people working in paid positions full-time or part-time.

In addition to paid staff, Catholic parishes large and small have numerous volunteers—parishioners involved in social ministries, catechists, leaders of Bible study or prayer groups, youth ministers, people who visit the sick or homebound, and so on. For Mass and other liturgical services, volunteers may include altar servers, musicians, choir members, readers, ushers or greeters, extraordinary ministers of Communion, and others.

PROVINCES AND STATE CATHOLIC CONFERENCES

Provinces

In the United States, two states have two Latin rite archdioceses and hence two ecclesiastical *provinces*—California, with the Archdioceses of Los Angeles and of San Francisco; and Texas, with the Archdioceses of San Antonio and of Galveston-Houston. In a number of the country's other more populous states, the ecclesiastical province is co-extensive with the state boundaries. New York

(Archdiocese of New York), New Jersey (Newark), Pennsylvania (Philadelphia), Florida (Miami), Ohio (Cincinnati), Illinois (Chicago), Michigan (Detroit), Indiana (Indianapolis) and Wisconsin (Milwaukee) are examples.

In other areas the dioceses of two or more states are united in a single province. For example, the Boston ecclesiastical province covers the other three dioceses in Massachusetts plus those in Maine, Vermont and New Hampshire; the St. Paul and Minneapolis province includes the four dioceses of North and South Dakota as well as the other dioceses in Minnesota.

The relationship of the archdiocese, or *metropolitan see*, to the dioceses under it (called *suffragan sees* in this context) rarely comes into play in news coverage. The limited authority an archbishop has over the other diocesan bishops in his province is largely in terms of internal church affairs. The bishops of a province meet periodically, for example, to discuss common policy on various pastoral matters and to draw up lists of priests who may be suggested to Rome as potential candidates to be made bishop.

State Catholic Conferences

As the public policy arm of a state's Catholic bishops, a state Catholic conference may often be in the news, especially if religious freedom or moral and social values espoused by the church are at issue in state executive or legislative proposals or judicial proceedings. In a few small states that have only one diocese, such as Vermont, New Hampshire and Rhode Island, there is no state Catholic conference, and the diocese itself has some form of public policy or government liaison office that deals with such issues. Most states, however, do have a state Catholic conference. Its headquarters are usually located in the state capital, even if that is not the most populous city or the seat of the most important diocese in the state. The New York State Catholic Conference, for example, is located in Albany, not New York City; the Catholic Conference of Ohio is in Columbus, not Cincinnati. Typically the bishops of the state are the members of the conference, but the executive director is a layperson, often someone with a background in law.

OTHER LOCAL CATHOLIC RESOURCES

Catholic Colleges and Universities

There are more than 230 Catholic colleges and universities in the United States, most of them sponsored by religious orders, though often governed by lay-majority boards. Their faculty, especially those in theology or religious studies departments, may be an important news resource not only on church issues but also on broader community issues with a moral or religious dimension, from medical ethics to prison reform, from immigration to capital punishment.

Catholic Seminaries

By its nature, a *theological seminary*—which offers a four-year postgraduate program in theology for future priests—will have on its faculty experts in Scripture, systematic theology, moral theology and ethics, historical theology, liturgy, sacramental theology, church history and a range of related disciplines. *College seminaries* are also likely to have experts in theology and other religious fields on their faculty.

Catholic Hospitals

Catholic health care institutions are bound by a code of ethical and religious directives established by the U.S. bishops. Doctors and other health care staff familiar with those directives and their application in complex situations can be a source of insight and expertise about church teachings on human life and dignity in areas where life and dignity face some of the greatest challenges.

Religious Orders

Every diocese has communities of men and women religious: monasteries, convents, priories or other religious houses. Many of those priests, brothers and nuns have academic and experiential backgrounds and areas of expertise that would surprise an outsider unfamiliar with the emphasis that religious orders have placed on education for their members.

Eastern Catholic Churches

Parishes of Eastern Catholic churches are spread throughout the United States, although most of them are in more urban areas. In many of these parishes the pastor or some of the parishioners may have extensive knowledge of their country of origin and expertise on the religious, political and cultural situation there. For example, in Detroit there is a large community of Chaldean Catholics, whose roots are in Iraq. Many Ukrainian and Ruthenian Catholics immigrated to Pennsylvania, New Jersey and Ohio, but there are Ukrainian and Ruthenian parishes scattered elsewhere across the country as well. It's worthwhile to find out what Eastern rite Catholic churches have a presence in your community and how they might serve as news resources.

Glossary of Church Terms

Here is a brief glossary of terms often used in the Catholic Church that may not be completely familiar to journalists who have not had a great deal of experience in covering church matters. One may hope that even more experienced journalists will find one or two new insights here. Terms are capitalized only if they are always capitalized. For example, *archbishop* is capitalized only when used as a title before a name, but *College of Cardinals* is a proper name in all uses—so the *archbishop* entry is lowercased but the other is capitalized.

annulment. Technically called a *decree of nullity*, an annulment of a marriage is a decision by a church court, confirmed by an appellate court, that a *putative marriage* was not valid from the start because something was lacking: full knowledge and consent by both parties, freedom from force or grave fear, or some other factor needed for a valid marriage. "Putative" (meaning apparent or seeming) is a key word in the entire process: It refers to a marriage in which at least one party acted in good faith, believing it was valid at the time it took place. Children from a putative marriage are considered legitimate even if the marriage is later ruled to be invalid. This has been a source of one of the major popular misunderstandings of annulments; namely, that an annulment somehow makes the children of that union illegitimate. Church law explicitly rejects this interpretation, saying that children of a putative marriage are legitimate even if the marriage is later judged to be invalid.

apostolic nuncio. Church term for the Vatican ambassador to another country and the papal liaison with the church in that country. An apostolic nuncio, also called a *papal nuncio*, is always an archbishop, and it is his religious title that is capitalized as a title before his name, e.g., *Archbishop Pietro Sambi, apostolic nuncio to the United States,* not *Apostolic Nuncio Pietro Sambi.* See **religious titles before names**. In a country with which the Vatican does not have diplomatic relations, the official Vatican liaison with the church there is called an *apostolic delegate.* Papal representatives in the United States were apostolic delegates until 1984, when full diplomatic relations were established. There was a brief period, from 1984 to 1991, when the Vatican ambassador to the United States was called the *pro-nuncio* because he was not the dean of the world's ambassadors to the United States (a position that under a Vienna convention is automatically given to the Vatican ambassador in many countries but in other countries is given to the senior foreign ambassador, wherever he is from). In 1991 the Vatican quit using *pro-nuncio* as the title for its ambassadors who were not deans of the ambassadorial corps and began calling all papal representatives with full rank of ambassador *nuncio*.

archbishop. The title given automatically to bishops who govern archdioceses. It is also given to certain other high-ranking church officials, notably Vatican ambassadors (apostolic nuncios: see that entry), the secretaries of Vatican congregations and the presidents of pontifical councils. *Adj.* **archepiscopal**.

archdiocese. The chief diocese of an ecclesiastical province (see *province* and *metropolitan*). It is governed by an archbishop. *Adj.* **archdiocesan**. See *diocese* and *archeparchy*.

archeparchy. The chief diocese of an Eastern Catholic ecclesiastical province. In most contexts it can be called an *archdiocese*, but if some legal distinction between Eastern and Latin Catholic jurisdictions is important, it may be necessary to introduce the term. The head of an archeparchy is called an *archeparch*, but in most contexts he can be called an *archbishop*. There are only two Catholic archeparchies in the United States: the Byzantine Catholic Archdiocese of Pittsburgh and the Ukrainian Catholic Archdiocese of Philadelphia. See *eparchy*.

auxiliary bishop. A bishop assigned to a Catholic diocese or archdiocese to assist its residential bishop. Whether in a diocese or archdiocese, his title is *bishop*.

bishop. The highest order of ordained ministry in Catholic teaching. Most bishops are diocesan bishops, the chief priests in their respective dioceses. But some (auxiliary bishops) are the top assistants to their diocesan bishops, and some priests are made bishops because of special posts they hold in the church, such as certain Vatican jobs. Diocesan bishops and their auxiliaries are responsible for the pastoral care of their dioceses. In some cases diocesan bishops are assigned a coadjutor bishop, who is like an auxiliary except that he automatically becomes the diocesan bishop when his predecessor resigns or dies. See ***auxiliary bishop*** and ***coadjutor***. In addition to their diocesan responsibilities, all bishops have a responsibility to act in council with other bishops to guide the church. *Adj.* **episcopal**.

bishops' conference. A national (or in a very few cases regional) body of bishops that meets periodically to collaborate on matters of common concern in their country or region, such as moral, doctrinal, pastoral and liturgical questions; relations with other religious groups; and public policy issues. It is also called an *episcopal conference*. The U.S. conference is the *United States Conference of Catholic Bishops*, or *USCCB*. See that entry.

brother. A man who has taken vows in a religious order but is not ordained or studying for the priesthood. Sometimes he is called a *lay brother* to distinguish him from clerical members of religious orders. See **lay**.

canon. Greek for rule, norm, standard or measure, it is used in several ways in church language. (1) The canon of Sacred Scripture is the list of books recognized by the church as inspired by the Holy Spirit. (2) Before the liturgical reforms of the Second Vatican Council, the single eucharistic prayer used universally in the Latin Mass was called the Roman Canon. Now that there are four eucharistic prayers in general use, they are usually referred to as Eucharistic Prayer I, II, III or IV, but they may also be called canons. The first of these is still called the Roman Canon because it is nearly identical to the original Roman Canon. (3) *Canon* is another name for a law in the *Code of Canon Law*. *Adj.* **canonical**. See also ***canon law***.

canon law. A code of ecclesiastical laws governing the Catholic Church. In the Latin or Western Church, the governing code is the 1983 *Code of Canon Law*, a revision of the 1917 *Code of Canon Law*. A separate but parallel *Code of Canons of the Eastern Churches*, issued in 1990, governs the Eastern Catholic churches. That document was the first comprehensive code of church law governing all Eastern Catholic churches.

cardinal. Highest-ranking Catholic clergy below the pope. By church law cardinals are regarded as the pope's closest advisors, and when a pope dies those who are not yet 80 years old meet in a conclave in Rome to elect a new pope. Most cardinals are archbishops; canon law since 1983 says they must at least be bishops, but exceptions have been made in several cases where a noted priest-theologian over the age of 80 has been named a cardinal to honor his theological contributions to the church. See **College of Cardinals**.

celibacy. Refers to a decision to live chastely in the unmarried state. At ordination, a diocesan priest or unmarried deacon in the Latin rite Catholic Church makes a promise of celibacy. The promise should not be called a "vow." *Adj.* celibate. See **chastity**.

chancellor. The chief archivist of a diocese's official records. Also a notary and secretary of the diocesan curia, or central administration; he or she may have a variety of other duties as well. It is the highest diocesan position open to women.

chastity. In its general sense chastity does not mean abstinence from sexual activity as such, but rather moral sexual conduct. Marital chastity means faithfulness to one's spouse and moral conduct in marital relations. The religious vow of chastity taken by brothers, sisters and priests in religious orders is a religious promise to God to live the virtue of chastity by not marrying and by abstaining from sexual activity. When diocesan priests and unmarried deacons make a promise of celibacy, they are not taking religious vows; their commitment to live chastely in an unmarried state should be described as a promise, not a vow. See **celibacy**.

church. Apart from its obvious use to refer to a building where Christians gather to worship God, *church* has a rich theological and doctrinal meaning for Catholics that also sets limits on how it is applied. The *local* or *particular church* means the (arch)diocese, the community of faithful gathered around the altar under its bishop. Each particular church has all the necessary means of salvation according to Catholic teaching—that is, fidelity to apostolic teaching, assured by ordained ministry in apostolic succession; the seven sacraments accepted throughout Christianity before the Reformation; and all the communal means to holiness that God grants through his graces. The *universal church*— the meaning of *catholic church*, lowercased—is the communion of all those particular churches spread throughout the world who are in union with the bishop of Rome and who share in fidelity to apostolic teaching and discipleship to Christ. Catholics also recognize the mainline Orthodox churches as churches; and until the recent ordination of women in several Old Catholic churches of the Union of Utrecht, the Catholic Church had recognized Union of Utrecht churches as churches. Christian churches which share partially in the historic apostolic communities of Christian discipleship, but which in the Catholic Church's perspective do not have the fullness of apostolic succession in their bishops or ordained ministry, are called *ecclesial communions*, rather than churches. This position, strongly affirmed by the world's Catholic bishops at the Second Vatican Council and reaffirmed in numerous church documents since then, remains a topic of considerable disagreement in ecumenical dialogues. In Catholic teaching the church embraces all its members—not only those still living on earth, but also those in heaven or purgatory. The ancient teaching that outside the church there is no salvation (*extra ecclesiam nulla salus*) has been officially nuanced in church teaching to include many who do not explicitly embrace the church and all its teachings, or even many who join no Christian religion. The teaching affirms the central role and responsibility of the church to reach out to all people with the Gospel message while acknowledging that those who have not been apprised or convinced of that message may still be saved if they live upright lives in accord with their own convictions and understanding of God.

clergy. In Catholic usage, a collective term referring to all those ordained— bishops, priests and deacons—who administer the rites of the church. *Adj.* **clerical**.

coadjutor. A bishop appointed to a Catholic diocese or archdiocese to assist the diocesan bishop. Unlike an auxiliary bishop—see ***auxiliary bishop***—he has the right of succession, meaning that he automatically becomes the new bishop when the diocesan bishop retires or dies. By canon law, he is also vicar general of the diocese. If the diocese is an archdiocese, he is called *coadjutor archbishop* instead of *coadjutor bishop*. In recent years a growing number of U.S. bishops in larger dioceses or archdioceses have requested and received a coadjutor in the final year or two before their retirement, in order to familiarize their successor with the workings of the (arch)diocese before he has to take over the reins.

College of Cardinals. A group of men chosen by the pope as his chief advisers. Most are heads of major dioceses around the world or of the major departments of the Vatican, or are retired from such posts. In the interregnum following the death of the pope, the College of Cardinals administers the church, and those under the age of 80 meet in a conclave to elect a new pope.

collegiality. The shared responsibility and authority that the whole college of bishops, headed by the pope, has for the teaching, sanctification and government of the church.

conclave. The gathering of the world's Catholic cardinals, after the death of a pope, to elect a new pope. Only cardinals under the age of 80 are allowed into a conclave under current church rules.

congregation. (1) A term used for some Vatican departments that are responsible for important areas of church life, such as worship and sacraments, the clergy, and saints' causes. (2) The proper legal term for some institutes of men or women religious, all of which are commonly called *religious orders*. The difference between a religious congregation and a religious order is technical and rarely of significance in news reporting. (3) Any gathering of Christians for worship.

consistory. A meeting of cardinals in Rome. It can be an *ordinary consistory*, attended only by cardinals in Rome at the time of the meeting, or an *extraordinary consistory*, to which all cardinals around the world are summoned.

curia. The personnel and offices through which (1) the pope administers the affairs of the universal church (the Roman Curia), or (2) a bishop administers the affairs of a diocese (the diocesan curia). The principal officials of a diocesan curia are the vicar general, the chancellor, officials of the diocesan tribunal or court, examiners, consultors, auditors and notaries. When referring to the Roman Curia, *Roman Curia* and *Curia* used alone are usually capitalized (like *Senate* when referring to the U.S. Senate), but *curia* is not capitalized in reference to a diocesan curia unless it is part of a full proper name.

deacon, diaconate. In the Catholic Church, the diaconate is the first of three ranks in ordained ministry. Deacons preparing for the priesthood are *transitional deacons*. Those not planning to be ordained priests are called *permanent deacons*. Married men may be ordained permanent deacons, but only unmarried men committed to lifelong celibacy can be ordained deacons if they are planning to become priests. *Adj.* **diaconal**.

defrocking. See *laicization*.

delict. The church term for a crime. Church crimes are spelled out in the *Code of Canon Law* for the Latin rite and in the *Code of Canons of the Eastern Churches* for Eastern Catholic churches.

diaconate. See *deacon*, *diaconate*.

dicastery. A church term for one of the major departments of the Roman Curia—the Secretariat of State, Vatican congregations, tribunals, pontifical councils and a few other departments. The term does not appear with this definition in most English dictionaries, which is part of the reason it is listed here. It ordinarily does not come into play in news coverage of the Vatican, but it may do so in certain limited contexts. Generally, it is more appropriate to refer to a Vatican dicastery by its more specific proper name: congregation, pontifical council, etc.

diocesan bishop. A bishop who heads a diocese. He may be assisted by auxiliary bishops or a coadjutor bishop (see *auxiliary bishop* and *coadjutor*). Also sometimes referred to as a *residential bishop*.

diocesan curia. The personnel and offices assisting the bishop in directing the pastoral activity, administration and exercise of judicial power of a diocese.

diocese. A particular church; the ordinary territorial division of the church headed by a bishop. The chief diocese of a group of dioceses is called an *archdiocese*; see that entry. *Adj.* **diocesan**.

Eastern Catholic churches. The Catholic churches with origins in Eastern Europe, Asia and Africa that have their own distinctive liturgical, legal and organizational systems and are identified by the national or ethnic character of their region of origin. Each is considered fully equal to the Latin tradition within the church. In the United States there are 15 Eastern church dioceses and two Eastern church archdioceses. In addition, there is one non-territorial Eastern church apostolate in the United States whose bishop is a member of the U.S. Conference of Catholic Bishops. See *archeparchy* and *eparchy*.

eparchy. Eastern Catholic equivalent to a *diocese* in the Latin Church. It is under the pastoral care of an *eparch* (bishop). Unless some legal distinction between a Latin rite diocese and an Eastern Church eparchy is relevant to a news report, in most cases it is appropriate to refer to an eparchy as a diocese and to its leader as a bishop. *Adj.* **eparchial**. See *archeparchy*.

episcopal. Refers to a bishop or groups of bishops, or to the form of church governance in which ordained bishops have authority.

episcopal vicar. A priest or auxiliary bishop who assists the diocesan bishop in a specific part of the diocese, over certain groups in the diocese, or over certain areas of church affairs. Some large dioceses, for example, are divided geographically into several vicariates or regions, with an episcopal vicar for each; some dioceses have episcopal vicars for clergy or religious or for Catholics of certain racial or ethnic groups. See *vicar general*.

excommunication. A penalty or censure by which a baptized Catholic is excluded from the communion of the faithful for committing and remaining obstinate in certain serious offenses specified in canon law. Even though excommunicated, the person is still responsible for fulfillment of the normal obligations of a Catholic.

faculty. Church authorization, given by the law itself or by a church superior, to perform certain official church acts. In some rare cases a member of the clergy will be denied certain faculties, such as hearing confessions or preaching during the liturgy, because of public positions taken that are not in accord with church teaching.

finance council. A diocesan body mandated by the *Code of Canon Law* that is charged with preparing the annual diocesan budget and annually reviewing diocesan expenses and revenues. The finance council must be consulted for financial transactions of a given dollar level undertaken by the bishop and must give its consent to transactions at another dollar threshold. The threshold amounts are established periodically by an agreement with the Holy See and are currently subject to annual inflation changes determined by the cost of living index.

hierarchy. In Catholic usage, the term is used most commonly to refer collectively to the bishops of the world or a particular region. In technical uses, however, it may refer to all those who are ordained: deacons and priests as well as bishops. In the canon law of the Eastern Catholic churches, *hierarchs* is a term regularly used to describe the bishops of a church when describing their collective authority or function.

Holy See. The primary official term of reference for the Diocese of Rome, as the chief diocese of Catholic Christendom; used to refer to the pope and the Roman Curia—congregations, tribunals, and various other offices—in their role of authority over and service to the Catholic Church around the world. In most news uses, *Vatican* is synonymous with *Holy See*: A Holy See representative is a Vatican representative, a congregation of the Holy See is a Vatican congregation, etc.

laicization. The process by which a priest is returned to the lay state. It is sometimes used as a penalty for a serious crime or scandal, but more often it comes at the request of the priest. A laicized priest is barred from all priestly ministry with one exception: He may give absolution to someone in immediate danger of death. The pope must approve all requests for laicization. When a priest is laicized without his consent, for a crime such as living in concubinage, committing child sexual abuse or using the confessional to solicit sex, it is sometimes called *defrocking* or *unfrocking*. Those terms, which are not used in church law, should be restricted to forcible laicizations, since they connote a penalty.

laity/lay. In canon law, anyone not ordained a deacon, priest or bishop is a layperson. In this legal sense women religious (sisters) and unordained men religious (brothers) are laity. In the documents of the Second Vatican Council, however, the laity are those who are neither ordained nor members of a religious order. The Vatican II sense is the one usually intended in most discussions of laypeople and their role in the church.

lay ecclesial ministry. Not a specific job title, but a general theological description of the work of Catholics who are not ordained but are engaged in substantial public leadership positions in church ministry, collaborating closely with the ordained leadership and working under their authority. In the United States well over 30,000 such lay ministers—an average of more than 1.6 per parish nationwide—are employed by Catholic parishes in full- or part-time positions of more than 20 hours a week. Among those who are in paid posts, about 40 percent are coordinators of religious education. Their other key ministries include general pastoral associate, youth minister, music minister, and liturgical planner or coordinator. Tens of thousands of other Catholics engage in volunteer lay ministry in U.S. parishes as catechists; as readers, altar servers, music leaders or other liturgical ministers; as social justice ministers; or in a variety of other health, charity, service or church-related ministries.

Ecclesial is reserved to those who are in church-recognized leadership positions, generally certified to represent the church in their area of expertise after appropriate human, spiritual, intellectual and pastoral formation. In a 2005 document, *Co-Workers in the Vineyard of the Lord*, the U.S. bishops encouraged the growth of lay ecclesial ministry and set out general guidelines for the formation and the recognition or certification of such ministers.

liturgy. The general term for all the church's official acts of worship. It includes the Mass (also called the *eucharistic liturgy*), the celebration of the other sacraments, and the Liturgy of the Hours, which contains the official prayers recited by priests and some others to sanctify parts of the day. See **Mass**, **sacraments** and **vespers**.

Mass. The central act of worship in the Catholic Church. In most Eastern Catholic churches the Mass is called the *Divine Liturgy*. The Mass is divided into two main parts. The Liturgy of the Word includes Scripture readings and a homily and ends with the general intercessions. The Liturgy of the Eucharist begins with the offering of the gifts, followed by consecration of the bread and wine and the reception of Communion. Catholics believe that in the consecration the bread and wine truly become the body and blood of Christ.

metropolitan. A *metropolitan see* is an archdiocese that is the chief diocese of an ecclesiastical province. The archbishop who heads that province is called the *metropolitan*, but usually only in contexts referring to him in his capacity as head of the province. See **province**.

ministry. A broad term in Catholic usage for any activity conducive to the salvation of souls. It can include ordained ministry such as liturgical leadership and administration of the sacraments, or lay ministry such as instructing children in the faith, serving the poor, visiting the sick, or being an altar server, reader or music leader at Mass. See **lay ecclesial ministry**.

monsignor. An honorary ecclesiastical title granted by the pope to some diocesan priests. Priests in religious orders or congregations never receive the title of monsignor. In English the standard abbreviation as a title before the name is *Msgr.* American publications vary in whether they use the abbreviation or the full word before the name in news reporting. In covering the church internationally, however, it is also important to realize that the Catholic Church and news agencies in many other nations use *Msgr.* or *Mgr.* as the religious title before the name of bishops and archbishops, not just before the name of priests who have received that honorary ecclesiastical title from the pope. Check on the Web or in other resources to determine whether the man in question is a bishop or just a priest who has an honorary title from the pope.

nun. (1) Strictly speaking, a member of a religious order of women with solemn vows. (2) In general, all women religious, even those in simple vows, who are more properly called *sisters*. Whether a woman religious is a nun or sister in a strict canonical sense, in news reporting it is appropriate to use the term *Sister* as the religious title before her name.

ordinary. A diocesan bishop or his equivalent, his vicar general and episcopal vicar, or a major superior of a clerical religious order, congregation or society. It refers to someone with *ordinary* authority in church law over a group of clergy, over certain pastoral concerns in a specific geographical area or over the members of a religious order. The term *ordinary* was formerly restricted to diocesan bishops and major superiors of religious orders, but it was expanded in the 1983 *Code of Canon Law* to include vicars general and episcopal vicars. It is not uncommon for bishops and other church officials schooled in the previous canon law code to use the term *ordinary* mistakenly to refer only to diocesan bishops or major superiors of men religious. If a church official uses the term in this more restricted former use, it is wise to question him or her on what he or she means by the term.

papal nuncio. See *apostolic nuncio*.

parish. A specific community of the Christian faithful within a diocese, having its own church building, under the authority of a pastor who is responsible for providing ministerial service. Most parishes are formed on a geographic basis, but they may be formed along national or ethnic lines.

pastor. A priest in charge of a Catholic parish or congregation. He is responsible for administering the sacraments, instructing the congregation in the doctrine of the church, and providing other services to the people of the parish. *Pastor* is not ordinarily used as a title before the name of a Catholic priest: He is *Father* John Smith or *Msgr.* John Smith or *the Rev.* John Smith, depending on your publication's style manual.

pastoral council. A parish or (arch)diocesan body that the pastor or (arch)bishop consults concerning policies and major decisions in the governance of the local church. Such a council's role is consultative and always subject to the final authority of the pastor or bishop.

presbyteral council. Also known as the *priests' council*, this is the principal consultative body mandated by the *Code of Canon Law* to advise the diocesan bishop in matters of pastoral governance. It consists of bishops and priests serving the diocese.

presbyterate. May be a synonym for *priesthood* or may refer to the collective body of priests of a diocese or similar ecclesiastical jurisdiction.

province. (1) A grouping of an archdiocese, called the *metropolitan see*, and the dioceses under it, called *suffragan sees*. The *Code of Canon Law* spells out certain limited obligations and authority that the metropolitan archbishop has with respect to the dioceses within his province. (2) A grouping of communities of a religious order under the jurisdiction of a provincial superior.

religious priest/diocesan priest. *Religious priests* are professed members of a religious order or institute. Religious clergy live according to the rule of their respective orders. In pastoral ministry, they are under the jurisdiction of their local bishop, as well as of the superiors of their order. *Diocesan*, or *secular*, *priests* are under the direction of their local bishop. Most serve in the parishes of the diocese, but they may also be assigned to other diocesan posts and ministries or be released for service outside the diocese.

religious titles before names. Of course you will follow your own publication's style manual for use of religious titles before names. But in general, Catholics refer to nuns as *Sister*, religious brothers as *Brother* and priests as *Father*, and those religious titles take precedence over whatever job titles they might hold, such as pastor, chancellor, vicar general, associate pastor, executive director. The other chief religious titles for clerics are *Msgr., Bishop, Archbishop, Cardinal, Pope* and, for the head of a male monastic community, *Abbot.* For many members of religious orders, the short version of their order's name may precede the religious title: *Mercy Sister Mary Smith, Jesuit Father John Smith, Benedictine Brother Peter Smith.* In certain cases it may be better to use an appositive phrase or some other approach: *Sister Janet Smith, a School Sister of Notre Dame*, rather than *School Sister of Notre Dame Sister Janet Smith.*

sacraments. Catholics, like Orthodox Christians, believe that there are seven sacraments: *baptism, confirmation, Eucharist, penance, matrimony, holy orders* and the *anointing of the sick*. The first three are also called the *sacraments of Christian initiation*, and in the Eastern Catholic and Orthodox traditions they are administered together in infancy. In the Latin rite Church baptism is administered to infants, but the first reception of the Eucharist (first Communion) and confirmation are typically delayed until the child has reached the use of reason, generally regarded as about the age of seven. Eastern Catholics and Orthodox usually refer to confirmation as *chrismation*. Penance is also called the sacrament of *reconciliation*. The anointing of the sick used to be called *extreme unction* when it was only given to those gravely ill or in danger of death. Now it can be administered to anyone who is seriously or chronically ill.

see. Another name for a diocese or archdiocese. It appears in such phrases as *Holy See, titular see, metropolitan see, suffragan see, see city*. The *see city* is that city after which the diocese or archdiocese is named. See **Holy See, metropolitan**, **province** and **titular see**.

seminary. An educational institution for men preparing for the priesthood.

sister. In popular speech, any woman religious. Strictly, the title applies to women religious of those institutes, mostly formed during or since the 19th century, whose members do not profess solemn vows. See **nun**.

superior. The head of a religious order or congregation. He or she may be the head of a province or of an individual house.

suspension. Church penalty under which a priest, while retaining his clerical status, is no longer permitted to perform priestly functions such as celebrating Mass, preaching or administering the sacraments.

titular see. If a bishop does not have his own diocese, he is given a *titular see*: that is, a place that once was the seat of a diocese but no longer is. Auxiliary bishops and bishops in Vatican service are examples of those given titular sees. Many titular sees are ancient cities of the Middle East or Northern Africa. But there are some titular sees in the United States as well, such as Bardstown, Ky. (original seat of what is now the Archdiocese of Louisville), or Jamestown, N.D. (now in the Diocese of Fargo). The *Annuario Pontificio* devotes more than 200 pages to the listing of titular sees, where it gives basic biographical information about the bishops who hold them.

tribunal. A *tribunal* (court) is the name given to the person or persons who exercise the church's judicial powers. Each diocese has a diocesan tribunal, used mainly to hear marriage cases. Each archdiocese has an archdiocesan tribunal—a court of first trial—and a metropolitan tribunal, an appeals court that reviews decisions of diocesan courts in that ecclesiastical province when necessary. (The Catholic Church in Canada has a slightly different system, with regional instead of metropolitan appeals courts.)

United States Conference of Catholic Bishops (USCCB). The national membership organization of the Catholic bishops of the United States, through which they act collegially on pastoral, liturgical and public policy matters affecting the Catholic Church in the United States. Episcopal conferences were recommended by the Second Vatican Council and have duties enumerated in the 1983 *Code of Canon Law* and the 1998 apostolic letter *Apostolos Suos*. The USCCB traces its origins to the 1919 establishment of the National Catholic Welfare Conference. In 1966, the conference was reorganized as the canonical entity known as the National Conference of Catholic Bishops and its twin civil corporation known as the U.S. Catholic Conference. Another reorganization in 2001 resulted in the USCCB.

vespers. Also called *evening prayer*, vespers is part of the Liturgy of the Hours, the series of psalms, prayers and readings for different parts of the day that Catholic priests and deacons are obligated to pray daily. Often a new bishop will present his letter of appointment to the priests of the diocese during a vespers service at the cathedral.

vicar general. A priest, auxiliary bishop or coadjutor bishop who assists the diocesan bishop in the governance of the entire diocese.

vow. A promise made to God with sufficient knowledge and freedom. Its purpose must be a moral good that, with God's grace, can be achieved. The promises spouses make to each other when they marry are vows. Men and women entering religious life take vows, typically of poverty, chastity and obedience. Celibacy is not a vow; it should be described as a promise.

Resources on the Church

DIRECTORIES

The *Official Catholic Directory*, published since 1817, is also widely known in church circles as the **Kenedy Directory** because of the publisher's imprint, P. J. Kenedy & Sons. It is an annual publication that lists every Catholic diocese, parish, mission, and educational, health care, or other official institution in the United States and its possessions, providing addresses, phone numbers and other information. It also lists every religious order and their headquarters and monasteries or community residences around the country. It tabulates data yearly, diocese by diocese and nationally, on the number of archbishops, bishops, priests, sisters, brothers, baptisms, first Communions, confirmations, marriages, students and teachers in Catholic schools, and numbers served by the church's health care and social services. In the back it has an alphabetical index of priests with their place of assignment, allowing the user to locate any priest in the country. It costs more than $300 but is a valuable tool for anyone who regularly has to contact priests, diocesan offices or other Catholic institutions and officials in all parts of the country. It can be ordered online at *www.catholicdir.com*.

The statistical tables of the *Official Catholic Directory* include church data from Puerto Rico, Guam and other U.S. territories and possessions where the bishops are not members of the USCCB (among such territories and possessions, only the bishop of the U.S. Virgin Islands is a USCCB member). Each year the **Center for Applied Research in the Apostolate (CARA)**, based at Georgetown University in Washington, recalculates the Kenedy data to determine the numbers for the dioceses of only those bishops who are part of the USCCB. CARA's figures reflect more accurately the data on what most people would think of as the U.S. Catholic Church. For CARA, phone 202-687-8080 or visit the Web site at *cara.georgetown.edu*.

If you need a tool like the Kenedy Directory only for the diocese or two in the area served by your publication, most dioceses publish their own diocesan directory annually with essentially the same information they provide to the national directory. Contact the communications director of your local diocese(s) to find out how to obtain such local directories.

Each spring USCCB Publishing produces a *Membership Photo Directory* of the U.S. Conference of Catholic Bishops. It has head shots of every bishop; biographical citations that in many cases include addresses, e-mail, and phone and fax numbers; a list of bishops by seniority; an alphabetical listing that includes each bishop's committee memberships; an alphabetical listing by diocese; breakdown by region; and lists of all USCCB committees with their current chairmen, members, consultants and staff. The 2007 directory costs $19.95. To order on the Web, go to *www.usccbpublishing.org* and click "church leadership" and "administration." Or phone 800-235-8722.

The *Directory of Catholic Communications Personnel*, published yearly by the USCCB Department of Communications, gives names and contact information for all U.S. diocesan and state Catholic conference communications directors, for USCCB and other national Catholic communications offices, and for key personnel in a number of other Catholic media offices, including some main Canadian and international offices. It is distributed free to journalists covering USCCB meetings. Contact the USCCB Office of Media Relations, 202-541-3200, to obtain a copy.

The *Directory of Lay Movements, Organizations and Professional Associations 2007-2009* is published by the USCCB Secretariat of Laity, Marriage, Family Life and Youth. It lists more than 100 such national Catholic groups with a brief description of each, names of leaders, phone numbers, mail and e-mail addresses, and Web sites. Contact the secretariat at 202-541-3040.

The **CARA** *Catholic Ministry Formation Directory* gives detailed contact and program information on U.S. Catholic institutions and programs that provide formation for the priesthood, for the permanent diaconate or for certified lay ministry. It is published every other year by CARA. The 2007 directory costs $75 and can be ordered online at *cara.georgetown.edu* or by phoning 202-687-8080.

Catholic News Service (CNS) has an online directory of all client U.S. diocesan newspapers, with phone listings and links to their Web sites. Go to *www.catholicnews.com* and click "CNS News Hub" and "Links to Client Publications." Or go directly to *newshub.cnslis.com/links-to-clients*.

The **Catholic Press Association (CPA)** has an online directory of U.S. and Canadian Catholic newspapers, magazines, newsletters and general publishers. Go to *www.catholicpress.org*. The CPA also publishes an annual

Catholic Press Directory with more detailed information about those publications. It costs $50 and can be ordered on the Web site.

OTHER RESOURCES ON THE CATHOLIC CHURCH

Catholic Almanac is an annual publication of Our Sunday Visitor, a large Catholic publishing house in Indiana. The 2007 edition costs $24.95. It includes highlights of news in the Catholic world from the previous year; summaries of Catholic teaching on faith, morality and social teaching; a glossary of Catholic terminology; an overview of church law, liturgy, sacraments, church history, and the organization of the church worldwide and in the United States, including a list of U.S. bishops; and articles on various aspects of the church and its work, such as Catholic religious life, apostolates, social services, education, communications, and ecumenical and interreligious relations. It can be ordered by phone at 800-348-2440 or online at *www.osv.com*. If you click "Books" and "OSV's Catholic Almanac" from the home page, you can also access portions of the almanac online, including its glossary.

Catholicism USA: A Portrait of the Catholic Church in the United States and *Global Catholicism: Portrait of a World Church*, both by Bryan T. Froehle and Mary L. Gautier of CARA (Maryknoll, N.Y.: Orbis Books, 2000 and 2003, respectively) are significant studies in Catholic demographics, practices and trends in the United States and the world. The former relies heavily on CARA's own extensive studies of U.S. Catholicism over the past four decades, the latter more on annual reports of the Vatican's Statistical Yearbook of the Church (*Annuarium Statisticum Ecclesiae*) since 1970 and on other national and international surveys and studies over those years.

CNS Stylebook on Religion: A Reference Guide and Usage Manual, third edition (Washington, D.C.: Catholic News Service, 2006), provides news reporters and writers with valuable practical descriptions and definitions of Catholic and other Christian terminology as well as background on other religions. It is geared toward helping journalists explain religious terminology to a more general readership that may include many people unfamiliar with that terminology. Among helpful appendixes are lists of Catholic religious orders by both names and initials, translations of the names of Vatican agencies and titles of Vatican officials, and descriptions of the structure of the USCCB. It is the official stylebook used by CNS and, with minor variations, by most of its publishing clients. The cost is $19.95. Phone 202-541-3250; mail Catholic News Service, Stylebook on Religion, 3211 Fourth Street NE, Washington, DC 20017-1194; e-mail *cns@catholicnews.com*; order online at *www.catholicnews.com/stylebook.htm*.

The *Catechism of the Catholic Church*, an official exposition of Catholic moral and doctrinal teachings, is a papally approved text that has been published in many languages. The normative Latin text has a 1994 copyright by Libreria Editrice Vaticana (LEV), which reserves the right to oversee all translations. For the English edition used in the United States, look for the *second edition*, with both a 1994 and 1997 copyright. (The 1994 translation used in the first English edition had numerous errors that were corrected in the second edition.) The most complete second edition is published by USCCB Publishing and contains more than 100 pages of supplemental material, including a glossary and an index of citations. Order online at *www.usccbpublishing.org*, or phone 800-235-8722. The USCCB administers the U.S. copyright for LEV. Doubleday also publishes a second edition, minus the supplemental material found in the USCCB's second edition. The official English text of the *Catechism*, including the glossary (but no indices), is also available online at *www.usccb.org/catechism/text*.

The Eastern Christian Churches: A Brief Survey by Ronald Roberson gives a clear, concise description of the history and the present situation of the Assyrian Church of the East and each of the Oriental Orthodox churches, Orthodox churches and Eastern Catholic churches. It is a must-read for anyone trying to sort out the complexities of the churches of the East, including the Eastern Catholic churches. The first six editions were published by the Pontifical Oriental Institute in Rome. The seventh edition is due in print in 2008, but the full text is online at *www.cnewa.org/generalpg-verus.aspx?pageID=182*. The online edition is regularly updated whenever new information, such as a change in a church's leadership, calls for it. Father Roberson, a Paulist priest, is the USCCB Secretariat of Ecumenical and Interreligious Affairs' associate secretary for Catholic-Orthodox relations and a former Catholic-Orthodox specialist at the Vatican's Pontifical Council for Promoting Christian Unity.

The **USCCB and Vatican Web sites**—*www.usccb.org* and *www.vatican.va*—carry extensive electronic documentation of their activities and statements on a wide range of issues. See the Vatican and USCCB chapters in this book for more details. Numerous other Catholic Web sites are also cited in those chapters.

The **USCCB Source Book**—*www.usccb.org/comm/source*—lists subject experts among USCCB staff on topics related to church life and ministry. It is produced by the USCCB Department of Communications as an aid for media seeking background and/or interviewees and for those seeking speakers for church meetings. Topics that the sources address relate to such matters as world and national affairs, church life, liturgy, priesthood and religious life.